Greek History

D0162263

Robin Osborne's energetic and lively guidebook is the ideal introduction to the study of ancient Greece, from the end of the Bronze
Age (*c.* 1200 BC) to the Roman conquest in the second century BC.

Covering all the most important topics in the study of the
Greek past, it also explores the different approaches to Greek
history – such as cultural, political, demographic and economic
– that students will encounter.

Professor Osborne sheds light on the full possibilities – and
problems – of working with the surviving evidence, by giving
examples from archaeological and art historical sources as well
as written texts.

The book also includes a clear and helpful guide to further
reading. It is an excellent starting point for those who want to
take their studies further.

Robin Osborne is Professor of Ancient History at the University
of Cambridge and a Fellow of King's College, Cambridge. His
books include *Greece in the Making c.1200–479 BC* (Routledge
1996), *Archaic and Classical Greek Art* (1998) and, with P. J.
Rhodes, *Greek Historical Inscriptions 404–323 BC* (2003).

Classical Foundations

The books in this series introduce students to the broad areas of study within classical studies and ancient history. They will be particularly helpful to students coming to the subject for the first time, or to those already familiar with an academic discipline who need orientation in a new field. The authors work to a common brief but not to a rigid structure: they set out to demonstrate the importance of the chosen subject and the lines of recent and continuing research and interpretation. Each book will provide a brief survey of the range of the subject, accompanied by some case studies demonstrating how one may go deeper into it. Each will also include guidance of a practical kind on sources, resources and reference material, and how to pursue the subject further. When complete, the series will comprise a critical map of the whole field of ancient studies.

The series is planned to include:

Early Christianity
Greek History
Greek Literature
Greek Philosophy
Late Antiquity
Latin Literature
Roman Social History
The Roman Empire

Books currently available in the series:

Roman Social History
Susan Treggiari

Latin Literature
Susanna Morton Braund

Greek History
Robin Osborne

Greek History

Robin Osborne

Routledge
Taylor & Francis Group

LONDON AND NEW YORK

First published 2004
by Routledge
11 New Fetter Lane, London EC4P 4EE

Simultaneously published in the USA and Canada
by Routledge
29 West 35th Street, New York, NY 10001

Routledge is an imprint of the Taylor & Francis Group

© 2004 Robin Osborne

Typeset in Times by
Florence Production Ltd, Stoodleigh, Devon

Printed and bound in Great Britain by
TJ International Ltd, Padstow, Cornwall

British Library Cataloguing in Publication Data
A catalogue record for this book is available from the
British Library

Library of Congress Cataloging in Publication Data
Osborne, Robin, 1957–
   Greek history/Robin Osborne.
     p.cm. – (Classical foundations)
   Includes bibliographical references and index.
   1. Greece – History – To 146 BC. I. Title. II. Series.

DF77. O67 2004
938–dc22   2003023355

ISBN 0–415–31717–7 (hbk)
ISBN 0–415–31718–5 (pbk)

Contents

Preface

That I should write this book was Richard Stoneman's idea, and he has waited for it patiently. Classics and history undergraduates unwittingly acted as a guinea-pig audience for the main text. Numerous colleagues over several years have equally unwittingly contributed to the view of Greek history that gets exposure here. Alastair Blanshard wittingly and willingly read a first draft and offered helpful suggestions for improvement. I am grateful to them all.

Abbreviations

dr.   drachma
FGH   F. Jacoby (1920–57) *Die Fragmente der griechischen Historiker*, Leipzig/Leiden.
ha.   hectare
IG   *Inscriptiones Graecae* (Berlin, Berlin Academy, 1873–   )
ML   R. Meiggs and D.M. Lewis (1969, with addendum 1988) *A Selection of Greek Historical Inscriptions to the End of the Fifth Century BC*, Oxford: Oxford University Press.
RO   P.J. Rhodes and R. Osborne (2003) *Greek Historical Inscriptions 404–323 BC*, Oxford: Oxford University Press.
W   M.L. West (1980) *Delectus ex Iambis et Elegis Graecis*, Oxford: Clarendon Press.

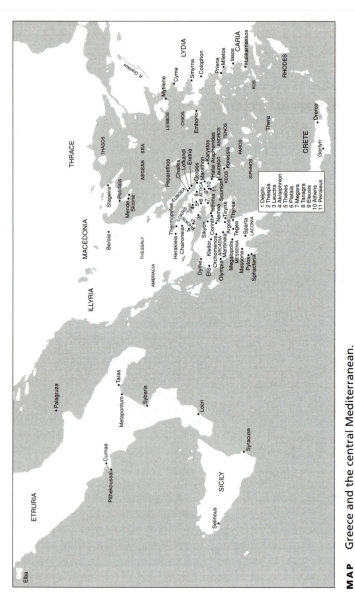

MAP Greece and the central Mediterranean.

Introduction

This book does not claim to tell anyone everything about (ancient) Greek history, but it does claim, to echo the title of the series in which it is published, to lay the foundations of the subject.

The foundations of history are not a sequence of dates and events, though there will be both dates and events enough in my account of Greek history. The foundations of history are a series of questions about how men relate to one another and to their environment over time. And those relations involve us. My opening questions are about how the ancient Greeks relate to us. Only once we appreciate how (dis)similar ancient Greek versions of familiar modern phenomena are – and one might choose warfare or education, but I choose athletics and courting – will we be alert to the need for constant vigilance about the assumptions which we necessarily import in order to sustain historical interpretation.

I proceed with questions about how we relate to the ancient Greeks, that is with questions about the sources from which we construct our histories of Greece. Whatever our historical interests we find ourselves piecing together a story from a mixture of contemporary writing, material remains, and later traditions. The material evidence can only be made to speak by creating contexts for each object: what any object 'meant' depends entirely on how it was used. This is familiar enough, and the reconstruction of contexts is the basic task of the archaeologist. But the same also applies to texts – not just to the fragments of poetry whose tone can be understood only if we know the occasion of their performance, but also to the later histories. We can only understand an ancient author's take on the past if we also understand what that writer or his informants' take on their present might be.

As we seek to control our own interpretations of source material there are a number of constraints which it is important that we do not overlook. My third chapter is concerned with those constraints, and above all with the human constraints imposed by the life expectancies and reproductive régimes of Greek men and women. Expectation of life at birth was short, and agricultural productivity was subject to extreme fluctuations as a result of climatic factors out of human control; one of the main debates among historians of ancient Greece has been about the extent to which the Greeks succeeded in insulating themselves against such natural factors. Just how well connected were the Greeks to other parts of the Mediterranean? What were the circumstances in which, and the expectations with which, they moved around that sea and settled in Sicily and Italy, in North Africa and around the shores of the Black Sea?

Natural, environmental and geographical constraints and opportunities only exist in relation to the attempts of living organisms to perform tasks. Aristotle in *Politics* famously stated that the polis existed not for life but for the good life. The fourth chapter looks at the ways in which the human actors in this world organised themselves into and as communities for purposes not simply of survival but survival in distinct forms. It looks at the evidence for tensions within communities and for their resolution variously through the development of conventions (law) and through the submission of the community to the charms and power of the charismatic individual.

Communities organised themselves not simply in the face of competing individuals within the community, and of their own and their environment's natural constraints, but in the face of competition with other communities. Chapter 5 looks at the ways in which conflicts between Greek cities were played out and at the extent to which those ways were challenged and changed by the advent of a threat that came not from another Greek community but from an outside power, the Persian empire. Living under a threat can transform a community even more than conquest itself would. The Persian threat profoundly changed the Greek world by forcing cities to join together in groups in order to resist and repel the danger. Chapter 6 looks at the changed dynamics of the fifth-century Greek world after the great Persian Wars of 480–479 BC, and argues for links between freedom and oppression not only at the level of the Greek city, where freedom from Persia came at the price of oppression by Athens or Sparta, but within the city, where the political freedoms of the citizen were not independent of the existence of widespread slavery.

Athens emerges both as the city which develops the most sophisticated means of oppressing other cities in the interests of continued resistance to Persia, and as a city whose political as well as economic life was heavily dependent on the use of non-Greeks as slave labour. But Athens was also the city in which the most extraordinary flowering of cultural life occurred, in literature, with tragic and comic drama, in philosophy, with the teaching of Socrates and the philosophical schools of Plato and Aristotle, and in the visual arts, with the sculptures of the Parthenon in the fifth century and the work of Praxiteles in the fourth. Chapter 7 stresses how diverse the experience of life was in different Greek cities, in terms of political or religious rituals and institutions and in terms of even basic modes of cultural expression (locally variant alphabets), and looks at the various ways in which the culture of the Greek city became more homogeneous over time.

The final chapter traces the political history of the fourth century down to and including the conquests of Alexander which created the basis for a Greek world that was geographically still more widespread but culturally more unified. The Macedonian conquest of Greece put an end to the oppression of one Greek city by another, both because of Macedon's overwhelming military

3

power and because Macedonian conquests outside Greece removed the potential for using international power politics to cajole cities into preferring subordination to the known quantity of another Greek city, rather than to the uncertain quantity of a foreign power. But for many Greek cities loss of an independent foreign policy was nothing new, and the characteristic life of the Greek city-state continued long after Philip of Macedon's establishment of the League of Corinth in 338 BC

This book is intended as a map of Greek history and of the issues that exercise scholars who study it. As a map its primary concern is with the user's orientation: it attempts not merely to give a view of Greek history, but to enable users to find their own way through Greek history. History is not something that has happened, but something which one makes for oneself. Because this is a map for use, I have concentrated on those areas where readers can readily launch themselves into Greek history with relative ease, that is areas where ancient literary source material is relatively easily accessible and can be made historical sense of with fairly minimal guidance. This has meant more concentration on Athens and Sparta and less concentration on Greek history after the end of the fourth century than a broad and equal survey would have afforded.

Like all maps, this map indicates only a limited number of dimensions and deliberately does not attempt to show everything. The Further Reading is intended to point the reader to places where the matters investigated here can be followed up with profit. It makes no attempt itself to constitute a bibliography of Greek history, but aims simply to put the reader in the way of works upon which I have myself drawn or which I have found useful in thinking about the topics discussed.

As archaeologists know to their costs, a variety of different structures may be built on identical foundations. If readers find themselves both enabled and challenged to build upon these foundations in a variety of different ways those foundations will have served their purpose.

FIGURES 1 and 2 Calyx Crater by Euphronios: Berlin Staatliche Museen F2180, from Capua, J.D. Beazley *Attic Red-figure Vases*, 2nd edition (Oxford, 1963) 13.1. Courtesy of Staatliche Museen, Berlin.

Chapter 1

Familiar but exotic

Why Greece needs history

What is going on in the scenes on this clay vessel, painted in Athens at the end of the sixth century BC? Taking our cue from the youth with the discus, we don't find too much difficulty in identifying this as a scene of athletes, in action, preparing for action, or tidying themselves up after action. One youth has apparently got a thorn in his foot and is having it pulled out. Another pours oil from a small flask into the palm of his hand ready to oil himself down. Another folds up his cloak or takes up a cloak he laid down folded earlier.

Athletics is the very activity that most readily links us to the ancient world: even those who cannot distinguish between the Greeks and the Romans know that some sort of ancient building is the appropriate thing to put on Olympic medals. It would, I think, be quite hard to find proverbial schoolboys who did not know that the Olympic games were named after a Greek festival which happened every four years at Olympia. Quite a lot of schoolboys will even know that the pentathlon is named after the Greek for 'five', the decathlon after the Greek for 'ten'. They may even know that there was a 'sacred truce' which interrupted wars so that the games could go on whatever the political relations between the cities from which the athletes came.

Now look a bit more closely at this pot. Start again with the discus-thrower. Just like the discus-thrower at the modern Olympics, is he? Well, no. After all, he is naked. We are pretty used to sculptures of naked discus-throwers: the Roman copy of a Greek bronze statue of a naked discus-thrower ('Discobolus') sculpted by Myron in the first half of the fifth century BC has been much copied in modern times, has inspired many images on medals for less exalted occasions than the modern Olympics, and has a familiar place in the history of film. But, however familiar the image of the naked discus-thrower has become, in modern western societies men do not do athletics naked. This is no trivial matter, for it indicates that one of the fundamental cultural boundaries was put in a different place.

Classical Greeks were themselves conscious that they were unusual in doing athletics naked, and one group of pot painters of the late sixth century added loincloths to the pots they painted for export to Etruria. Thucydides (1.6.3–6) inserts the practice of naked athletics into his very up-beat opening section of his history of the Peloponnesian War in which he sets out to prove that fifth-century Greeks were superior both to Greeks of earlier periods and to non-Greeks: it is only a matter of time, he implies, and everyone will take up this Greek invention (and there is a similar ring to Plato's allusion to the practice in *Republic* 5, 452c). By the second century AD, when Pausanias was visiting Greek sites, Greeks were explaining the practice with a story of a man whose loincloth fell off while he was racing, and Pausanias (1.44.1; compare *IG* vii 52) cannot have been the only person who interpreted the move to nakedness in functionalist terms: one can run faster without a loincloth. (Not surprisingly this is a piece of experimental archaeology that modern scholars have not been able to resist, solemnly timing their exhibitionist displays of sprinting along Greek beaches.) Isidore, bishop of Seville, writing in the seventh century AD, has a different functionalist explanation (*Etymologies* 18.17.2): after a runner's loincloth came adrift and he tripped, fell and died, nakedness was required to prevent further accidents.

Both these stories serve to familiarise doing athletics naked. The practice may be unfamiliar, but the reasoning that leads to it is recognisable: whether we think in terms of it enabling athletics to be done better, or whether we think in terms of the prevention of nasty accidents, the end aimed at remains the end aimed at in modern competitions – record times and distances, with the dangers of being hurt in the process minimised. The strange practice of doing athletics naked only serves to show that they were like us really. For E.N. Gardiner, writing in 1930, naked athletics achieved exactly what the doctor (then) ordered (1930: 57–8).

But these two stories are not the only ways in which the nakedness of Greek athletes has been regarded. Some modern scholars, for instance, have thought the Greek practice not an admirably rational response to perceived hazards of running in a loincloth, but rather quite irrational. How could an athlete possibly run at top speed if his genitals were flopping around? Roman observers, on the other hand, saw the practice not so much as irrational as immoral. The first of the great Roman epic poets, Ennius, said that 'to bare bodies among citizens is the beginning of vice', and the passage of Cicero that quotes and approves Ennius' statement expresses the view that love between men and boys began in the gymnasia where homoerotic affairs were permitted and unrestricted (*Tusculan Disputations* 4.70).

The link between athletics and sexual relationships between men and youths is not a product merely of a fevered Roman imagination. The so-called second book of the archaic poet Theognis of Megara includes the following couplet: 'Happy is he who, being in love, when he has come home spends time in the gymnasium, sleeping all day with a handsome boy' (2.1335–6, W), and the link between athletics and love is brought out on a number of Athenian red-figure pots. One such is the recently published cup attributed to the Carpenter Painter, where the exterior scenes show older men and youths engaged in a variety of athletic activities, while the interior shows a bearded man and a youth embracing.

The heteroerotic and homoerotic sex appeal of the sporting body, whether male or female, is not unfamiliar in modern western societies. It would be possible indeed, to make the Greeks seem rather like us by stressing the fantasies that get recorded in myth and also in anecdote about the attractions of women athletes (like the mythical Atalanta, beaten in a race for her hand in marriage only because unable to resist stopping to pick up the golden apples dropped by her opponent) or the illegal presence of women spectators at male athletic competitions (one Kallipateira revealed herself as a woman illegally spectating at the Olympic games when in her excitement at the victory of her son she leapt over the fence to congratulate him and revealed herself, Pausanias 5.6.7). To acknowledge that the sexual desire unleashed by the athlete might be heterosexual as well as homosexual is indeed important, but it should not be allowed to obscure the fact that the particular mode of sexual expresson regularly displayed, not just in fantasy but in reality, in the Greek *gumnasion* took a form likely to shock in two respects: its concentration on the male genitals and its concentration on boys.

Look again at Euphronios' pot. More particularly, take a look at the figure at the far left of one side, a figure I passed over in my earlier description. This is a young man, attended by his implausibly small boy slave, who holds a lace or thong in his right hand and with his left appears to be stretching the foreskin of his penis. Precisely the image to make the film censor limit viewing to those over eighteen. What is going on here? Modern scholars have often termed it 'infibulation', and the most thorough study is in a book by a remarkable figure, E.J. Dingwall, published in 1925 and entitled *Male Infibulation*, but no fibula is involved and recent treatments have preferred the term 'ligaturing'. In antiquity the practice was sometimes termed the dog-leash, *kynodesme*, and is first alluded to in a partially preserved satyr play by Aeschylus (the *Theoroi* or *Isthmiastai*, frg. 78a Radt, lines 28–31). The athlete is about to tie up his penis (or just possibly has recently untied it). Scholars who worry about the practicality of running naked discuss this practice, seen on a number of pots, in terms of 'genital protection', but the images on vases make it clear that the dog-leash was part of the discourse of sexuality and not merely of sensible precautions against damage to a vital part of the body.

There certainly are images of athletes with their genitals clearly tied up, sometimes with a neat bow, but pot painters do not restrict displays of the restrained male genitals to athletes, they also show the phenomenon in the case of revellers and satyrs. This is important not because it offers us a snapshot of real life – there were no real-life satyrs and the manner in which ligaturing is shown in some of these pots defies physiological possibility – but because the painters have adopted the ligatured male genitals as a sign in a discourse, a discourse which, by looking at the whole array of pots on which the sign appears, we can read. Even if we could persuade ourselves that it was the physical boisterousness of revellers that led them to tie themselves up, the juxtaposition on an early fifth-century wine-cooling vessel (*psykter*), now in the British Museum and attributed to the painter Douris, of a ligatured satyr with other satyrs displaying what sexual excitement enables a male to do with a pot, makes it clear that ligaturing carried a message about sex, and in particular about sexual restraint. But advertising sexual restraint only makes sense in circumstances in which loss of sexual restraint might be expected: by drawing attention to his self-control the ligatured athlete advertises the gymnasium as a place in which encounters and activities could be expected to have a sexual aspect.

Satyrs' sexual desire is most regularly for females; only rarely are they shown on pottery desiring each other or desiring young men. The erotic encounters of the symposium and of the revelling that followed it were similarly most frequently shown to be heterosexual. But the gymnasium, like athletic festivals themselves, was a space limited to men and boys. When pot painters show athletic victors being rewarded with garlands and the like it is always a bearded man who gives the victory tokens and it is always a boy who receives them. On one cup, once in Dresden but now lost, such a giving of prizes is juxtaposed with the handing over of other tokens of love, rabbits and the like, by an older man to a youth.

The very term pederasty, directly derivative of the Greek term *paiderastia* (love of boys), has become so associated with child abuse that it is hard to discuss Greek practice without explicitly or implicitly commenting on current sexual morality. Scholarly discussion of Greek homosexuality has exploded since the 1970s, but scholars have very largely avoided the issue of sexual relations with minors, despite the fact that it is relations between early teenage young men and older men with mature beards that lies at the heart of the visual evidence for homosexual relationships in Athens (in textual discussions the age of the parties is more often obscure).

Kenneth Dover, whose *Greek Homosexuality* of 1978 is the keystone of the field, was apt to explain relations between older and younger men in Athens with reference to the courting of young women by men in modern societies: 'No great knowledge of the world is needed to perceive the analogy between homosexual pursuit in classical Athens and heterosexual pursuit in (say) British society in the nineteen-thirties', he writes (p. 88), but when he comes to spell out the analogy we find that it is heterosexual courtship of young women by *young* men that he has in mind: 'In a heterosexual society a young man is not merely excused by his peers and elders if he pursues women with an intent to seduce' and again: 'Parents are therefore apt to issue different commands (explicit or implicit) to their sons and to their daughters ... If my son seduces my neighbour's daughter ...' (all p. 88). When Dover does discuss the fact that the object of passion is regularly referred to as *pais*, a child, it is the use of this phrase to refer to youths in their late teens that he devotes most attention to. Michel Foucault, whose whole project on the history of sexuality was premised on a conviction that past and present sexual practices were not comparable but contrasting, nevertheless exploits the same analogy in only a slightly more subtle way when he writes in *The Use of Pleasure*, volume 2 of *the History of Sexuality*, that

Later in European culture, girls or married women, with their behavior, their beauty, and their feelings, were to become themes of special concern . . . It seems clear, on the other hand, that in classical Greece the problematization was more active in regard to boys, maintaining an intense moral concern around their fragile beauty. (pp. 213–14).

Although Foucault's chapter is entitled 'A boy's honor', the issue of age is never there addressed, and the discussion earlier (pp. 199–200) of the age of the beloved concentrates on the question of the point at which the boy became too *old*.

These 'familiarizing' tactics must be resisted. In the discussion of love in his dialogue *Symposium*, Plato has Aristophanes give a speech in which he traces sexual attraction back to a splitting of what had once been a single organism, and stresses that those sliced from an original that was wholly male will 'so long as they are boys' show affection for men, but 'when they reach manhood they become lovers of boys' (191e–192a). The courtships to which the gymnasium played host were between mature men and immature boys, from the beginnings of puberty until the stiffening of the downy beard. Eighteen-year-olds were on the way out, or at least on their way to courting rather than being courted.

Two further points are important here. The first is that, despite that speech of Aristophanes in the *Symposium*, homoerotic desire was not regarded as restricted by nature to certain men, nor something that excluded heterosexual desire. The reputation of Alcibiades, the aristocratic degenerate *par excellence* in the history of classical Athens, shows this well enough. He too appears in the *Symposium* and there tells of his unsuccessful attempt to seduce Socrates – itself an outrageous turning of the conventional tables in which the younger man tries to seduce the older. But he also acquired a reputation for taking prostitutes, both free and slave, home with him (his wife did not much appreciate this behaviour, [Andokides] 4.14).

The second point is that we are not dealing merely with a difference with regard to male homosexual relations. Puberty was the beginning of sexual life for girls as well as for boys. The fifth-century laws preserved from Gortyn on Crete specify that an heiress may marry at 12, and in Xenophon's dialogue on house-hold management Ischomachus says that his wife was not yet 15 when he married her (*Oikonomikos* 7.5). Aristotle *Politics* 7.16 (1335ª6–35) has a long explanation of the physiology of repro-duction, leading to the recommendation that the best age for a woman to be yoked together with a man, to use the Greek imagery of marriage, was 18 (and 35 for the man), but this is a matter of quality of offspring, not of sexual morality. Once a girl or a boy reached puberty they became an appropriate object of sexual desire and sexual pursuit, though the pursuit took different forms in each case.

Athenian expectations and practices when it came to sexual behaviour were not just a more liberal version of contemporary western expectations and practices. Sexual behaviour in Athens was very far from unregulated, but the regulations have at best a superficial resemblance to contemporary laws on sexual be-haviour. Questions of age arise in Athenian law in connection with the requirement that those who have charge of youths in various capacities be over the age of 40, but the capacities of which we know this to be true are training boys for perform-ance in dithyrambic choruses at Athenian festivals ([Aristotle] *Constitution of Athenians* 56.3), and having charge of boys doing their military service aged 18 to 20 ([Aristotle] *Constitution of Athenians* 42.2) – both laws made in the fourth century but plau-sibly inherited from traditional practice. Questions of consent are simply not involved in the regulation of sexual behaviour at all, even in the case of heterosexual rape, and the distinction between what is allowable in public and what in private does not feature in law. Neither male nor female prostitution, as such, was against the law in Athens (indeed both were activities taxed by the city), but hiring out a boy over whom one had authority as a prostitute was illegal. But a citizen or citizen-to-be who of his own accord took money to perform sexual acts with another man was debarred from speaking in public. When it comes to conventions, rather than law, it is clear that the control of sexual desire, as of other appetites, was the central concern. Whether sexual desire was for women or for boys was not an issue. As already observed, pot painters who use satyrs to explore the limits of acceptable sexual behaviour primarily concentrate on their desire for women and for auto-stimulation.

If we return to the site of athletics, two texts bring out well the limits to the familiarity of the scene (as well as the variation in practices within the Greek world from place to place and time to time). The beginning of Plato's *Charmides* has Socrates returning from serving as a soldier at Potidaia in the northern Aegean and seeking company and the latest news in the *palaistra*, the wrestling school, something much closer to the modern 'gym' than the ancient *gumnasion*. Among the news that he seeks is news of the latest beauties, and his question is answered by the appearance of Charmides surrounded by a crowd of admirers: 'when I came to observe the boys I noticed that none of them, not even the smallest, had eyes for anything else, but that they all gazed at him as if he were a statue' (154c). Socrates then contrives to get Charmides to come and sit next to him and tells of the effect that Charmides' presence has on him, an effect redoubled when 'I saw inside his cloak and caught fire, and could possess myself no longer' (155d). Compare to that the gymnasiarchy law from Beroia in Macedonia, from the early second century BC. This long law covers all aspects of what the *gumnasiarch*, the civic official with overall charge of the *gumnasion*, is obliged to do and what should and should not happen in the *gumnasion*. One section of the law deals with the question of who can attend the *gumnasion*: slaves are not to be allowed, nor freedmen, nor their sons; nor are persons who have not been through the wrestling school, or persons engaged in a market trade; nor are the drunk or the mad. Nor are *paiderastai*. The *gumnasion* was a place in which status was asserted and negotiated, a place in which young men drew attention to their sexual desirability and older men responded eagerly but with a display of sexual control. It was a place elaborately governed by what

Jack Winkler termed protocols, the unspoken premises that were the fundamental conventions of citizen life.

It has been useful to emphasise the extent to which athletics was the site of sexual display in order to bring out just how strange we would find it if we strayed into the company of Greek athletes. It isn't hard to see now what is otherwise pretty puzzling – why the drinking vessels, bowls for mixing wine, sophisticated wine-coolers, and the rest of the equipment of the urbane party, should be thought appropriately decorated with pictures of athletes. The *symposion* and the revelling that followed were, after all, and as our references to Plato's description of one particular party in the *Symposium* have shown, the places in which sexual relations were further negotiated. But even in the Greek city, taking part in athletics was not solely about getting picked up. Indeed the emphasis in our visual and literary sources upon the youthfulness of athletes is something of a distortion of reality, a distortion arguably linked to the observable reluctance of classical Greek art to show bearded men naked. If the wrestling-schools were places for young men to hang out, athletic competition belonged elsewhere, and in particular it belonged to the religious festival.

The modern Olympic games circulate around major world cities, but the ancient Olympics were fixed in one place: the sanctuary of Zeus at Olympia in the valley of the river Alpheios in the western Peloponnese. Olympia was not at all a major city, and even Elis, in whose territory Olympia was in the classical period, was not one of the major players in Greek politics. One did not have to pass through Olympia in order to get anywhere else, despite the convenience of the river valley for transport: there simply is no place worth going to that can be reached by passing through Olympia. The explanation currently most popular among scholars as to why the sanctuary of Zeus at Olympia should have become so important at such an early date (certainly the eighth century, even if not the canonical date of 776 BC) is in fact precisely that it lay outside the power of any major city. Olympia was a place where members of city élites could meet and compete with each other precisely because it was not itself claimed by the powerful élite of a particular city as their prime place of local competition and display. Olympia shared with other great festival centres at which Greeks from different cities gathered, such as Delphi and Delos, the advantage that it was not the marker of a political territory.

Whatever the reason for its rise to popularity, surviving remains reveal that Olympia shot to prominence in the eighth century. Not only do numbers of small dedications rise dramatically, with terracotta figurines increasing from 21 in the ninth century to 837 in the eighth, but large numbers of very large dedications of bronze tripod cauldrons are made in the eighth century. These vessels seem to have been imported in finished form, which makes it unlikely that only successful athletes dedicated them. Rather the rise of the athletic games at Olympia seems to be part of a more general development of the sanctuary as a site of competition, of which competitive dedication is archaeologically the most visible part.

What good did making a dedication at Olympia do for anyone? If individuals were going conspicuously to expend significant amounts of wealth, were they not better off doing so in their own cities? One of the remarkable features of the Olympic festival is that it managed to establish itself as a place that could not be ignored: glory won at Olympia had to be recognised at home. The impossibility of ignoring Olympia is both illustrated and reinforced by the stories that are told about successful athletes there. Oibotas of Dyme in the northern Peloponnese, for instance, supposedly a victor in the middle of the eighth century, was sufficiently upset by not receiving due recognition that he laid on the Achaians a curse that is supposed to have prevented any Achaian from winning at Olympia until he received proper honour in 460 BC (Pausanias 7.17).

Winning at Olympia notoriously won you only a crown of olive (Herodotus 8.26.3), but it did much more than that. Cities 'topped up' the prizes that Olympic victors received: Solon is said to have been responsible for having Athenians who were

17

Olympic victors given 500 drachmas, victors in the Isthmian games at Corinth 100 dr. Plutarch, who tells us this (*Solon* XX), claims that at that time a sheep was worth a drachma. And at festivals other than the Olympic, Pythian, Isthmian and Nemean games, which formed a 'circuit', victorious athletes could in any case reckon to receive prizes of real value. In Athens itself victors at the Panathenaic games were given amphoras of oil for success in individual athletic events, oxen (for sacrifice) for victory in team events, and, by the fourth century at least, gold crowns and cash prizes of up to 1,500 dr. in value for victory in musical events. Outstanding athletes could go from festival to festival for a decade or more acquiring great wealth as well as great glory. It was indeed possible to be, in effect, a professional sportsman.

One of the most famous of such athletes was Theagenes, properly Theugenes, of Thasos, who won the boxing at one Olympics, the pankration at the next, the boxing at the Pythian games three times, nine victories at the Nemean games, ten at the Isthmian games, and the long-distance running at games at Phthia in Thessaly. In all, Pausanias goes on to tell us (6.11.5), he won 1,400 contests; Plutarch (*Moralia* 811e) makes it 1,200, an inscription from Delphi 1,300, but the general message is clear enough.

If Theagenes seems like so many modern sporting superstars, the stories told about him don't belong to the same genre that such modern heroes attract. For a start, they reveal a particular sense of fair play: Pausanias tells of Theagenes being fined heavily at Olympia not because of any foul during the boxing match but because he had entered it only out of malice to another, almost equally remarkable, competitor, Euthymos of Locri (Pausanias 6.6.5–6). But he also goes on to tell of the powers that Theagenes' statues had: after a statue had fallen on and killed someone who, out of hatred of Theagenes, had flogged it, the decision of the people of Thases to discard the statue led to a crop failure that ceased only when the statue was recovered and rededicated (Pausanias 6.11.2–9). Pausanias claims that statues of Theagenes elsewhere both within and outside the Greek world were worshipped and held to cure diseases.

Athletic victors come to occupy precisely the space between what we would call history and what we would call myth. That same Euthymos, defeated by Theagenes in the boxing at the seventy-fifth Olympics but victorious at the seventy-fourth and seventy-sixth, was, like Theagenes, reckoned to be the son not of the man whose patronymic he carried but of a supernatural father, in this case a river. What is more, he was said to have fought and defeated a Hero who had demonised Temesa since the time of Odysseus. This Hero had been one of Odysseus' companions who had been stoned to death after having raped a girl when drunk, and had had to be placated with a beautiful maiden each year – the maiden Euthymos falls in love with and marries, of course (Pausanias 6.6.4–11).

Winning at religious festivals brought a man the attention of the gods, and ever after the gods could be expected to look after him. Plutarch (*Moralia* 639e) tells us that at Sparta a place was reserved in the ranks next to the king for victors in the crown games. He further alleges that cities were expected to tear down part of their walls to welcome home an athletic victor, since a city with men of such a sort to fight for it does not need walls. In the early fifth century it was an Olympic victor, Eualkides, who commanded the Eretrian ships sent to assist the Ionians in their revolt from Persia in 499 (Herodotus 5.102), and it was a Pythian victor who was in charge of the ships sent by Croton to assist the Greeks at the battle of Salamis in 480 (Herodotus 5.47). Olympic victors were not always successful, but even in defeat they receive special treatment: Philippos has a career in which he gets banished from his home city, loses the bride of his choice, sails off to Cyrene and then from there voluntarily joins an attempt by Dorieus of Sparta to found a new city in western Sicily. He dies in the attempt, but because of his good looks the very people he was fighting against erected a hero's shrine on his tomb and offered cult to him.

The kudos of athletic victory could provide a platform not only for a military role or the ascent into mythical status but for practical political action. The Kylon who attempted to seize power at Athens in a political coup in the late seventh century was an Olympic victor and, told by the Delphic oracle that he should choose the great festival of Zeus for seizing the Acropolis at Athens, he assumed that that meant that he should choose the first day of the Olympic festival. He failed because there was also a great festival of Zeus in Attica: he got the moment wrong but his followers' deaths brought a curse upon those responsible (the curse of the Alkmaionidai: Thucydides 1.126.3–11).

A hundred years later Olympic success brought death to another man at Athens, this time the Athenian Kimon. Kimon had been banished by Peisistratos, the tyrant of Athens, off and on from c.560 to c.527. As an exile he still entered the chariot race at the Olympics and won, not once but twice in succession. On the second occasion he waived his victory in favour of Peisistratos himself, and in return he was allowed to return to Athens. But when he won a third time Peisistratos' sons had him murdered. The four mares with which he achieved all three victories were buried opposite him (Herodotus 6.103).

Skipping forward a further hundred years to the end of the fifth century, we find yet another attempt to make political use of Olympic victory. Alcibiades entered not one but seven chariots at the Olympic games in 416 and secured first, second and fourth (or perhaps even third) place – an unprecedented achievement. Thucydides gives us this information in his version of the speech which Alcibiades delivered in 415 when he tried, successfully, to persuade the Athenians to undertake a massive military expedition against Syracuse (Thucydides 6.16.1–2). Alcibiades opens that speech with a claim that he has more right to command and is worthy of it because of the glory he brought to Athens by his Olympic victories.

These sorts of claims did not go uncontested: there was a backlash to all of this. 'What benefit to his native city is a man who has wrestled well or is swift of foot or has thrown the discus or struck someone a fine blow on the jaw and carried off a prize?' asks a character in Euripides' lost play *Autolykos*, 'Do they fight the enemy with discuses in their hands or do they expel the enemy from their homeland by striking with their fist through the shields?' (Euripides fr. 441 Nauck). Nor was Euripides the first to voice such sentiments: Athenaeus, who preserves that quotation for us, traces the criticisms back to the poet and philosopher Xenophanes at the end of the sixth century who pointed out that producing successful athletes did not guarantee a city good laws (Xenophanes frg. 2 W; Athenaeus *Deipnosophistae* 413f–414c).

Part of this backlash is evidently the backlash of mind against body, a sort of intellectual snobbism. Part is a class matter. This itself cuts both ways: on the one hand athletics, and most of all chariot racing, was something that demanded leisure and money, something simply not available to those of low status – we have seen the formal official expression of that in the gymnasiarchy law at Beroia, which bans from the *gumnasion* those who practise the trades of the agora. On the other hand, fleet-footedness and packing a good punch were not respecters of birth, and men of relatively lowly background could potentially shine as athletes (hence, perhaps, all those athlete stories about the putative father not being the real father – could a good athlete really be low-born?). For such men to aspire to the condition of the well-born was itself a source of resentment, as we see in a further passage of one Achaios of Eretria also quoted by Athenaeus (*Deipnosophistae* 414d), where the objection is that the athlete behaves as if used to a life of luxury at home.

It is no more difficult for us to understand these criticisms than to work out that the youths on Euphronios' pot are engaged in athletics. But it is precisely because of the easy familiarity we feel with these and so many other activities and motifs that we come across in Greek art and Greek literature that we need Greek history: we need always to realise that the familiar discus-thrower is the inhabitant of a world in which the successful boy athlete expects to enjoy sexual relations with an older man and to grow up to be ascribed powers to heal and to protect his city from its enemies simply by his presence. Art history has traditionally said: 'Never mind the content, just look at the form.' Literary studies

21

always work to a canon. It is the historian's job to draw attention to the personal, social, political and indeed moral issues behind the literary and artistic representations of the Greek world. The historian's job is to present pederasty and all, to make sure that, in the comfortable analysis of a culture so like our own, we come face to face with the way the glory that was Greece was part of a world in which many of our own core values find themselves challenged rather than reinforced.

Chapter 2

Inventing the Greek polis

Shortly before the middle of the eighth century BC some Greeks decided to settle on the island of Ischia, which they came to call Pithekoussai, off the bay of Naples. This wasn't the first time Greeks had been in the area: Mycenaean pottery has been found at the western tip of the small island. But, to the best of our knowledge Greeks had not been present there during the eleventh, tenth, or ninth centuries. Settlement there in the middle of the eighth century follows renewed contact between Greece and Italy. The earliest signs of such contact come at the end of the ninth and beginning of the eighth century in the Tiber valley, where Greeks came across Etruscan communities which, both in material culture and in social formation, were at least as sophisticated as the Greeks themselves. Settling at Pithekoussai gave the Greeks a staging post for further contact with the Etruscans and with other people in the area.

Archaeological remains show very clearly that Pithekoussai proved an attractive place to settlers from various parts of Greece. Over the last fifty years, part of the acropolis, part of a very large cemetery, and part of a metal-working site have been excavated, and have revealed a large and diverse community. On the basis of the number of tombs excavated, and the area of the cemetery left unexcavated, the population of Pithekoussai by the end of the century has been estimated at between 5,000 and 10,000 people (see further, ch. 3 below). There is some sign of eighth-century agricultural establishments elsewhere on the volcanic and fertile island, but there is little doubt that the community at Pithekoussai could only grow so large because it could acquire food from elsewhere by virtue of the large number of ships that visited it.

What the visiting ships took away from Pithekoussai cannot be demonstrated archaeologically. We can trace Etruscan objects in Greek sanctuaries from the eighth century on, and no doubt some of these were dedications by returning sailors. But what the core items of exchange were remains subject to dispute. The most likely item remains metals. Etruria, and particularly north Etruria, were rich in metals, as was the island of Elba, and there is sign of some smelting of iron ore taking place on Pithekoussai itself. The eighth century is the period when iron replaces bronze as the main working metal in Greece, and demand for both iron and bronze was undoubtedly lively. Etruria could provide both copper, iron, and some tin, and a base in the western Mediterranean offered the possibility of participating in the major trade carrying tin, the vital ingredient that turns too soft copper into durable bronze, from Cornwall.

What the archaeology does reveal is something of the social organisation and cultural life of Pithekoussai. Pithekoussai was a cosmopolitan place. Although pots made on one Greek site might be carried by ships originating in and manned from another Greek site, the presence of significant quantities of pottery from Corinth, Euboea and Rhodes is suggestive of a mixed community. There is also evidence that some Phoenicians, who were themselves busy settling in Sicily, Spain, Sardinia and North Africa during the eighth century, were amongst the residents. Whatever the origin of the residents, the cemetery suggests that they behaved as a community with community customs. Graves are organised in family plots, and the rituals attendant on death depended upon the age and status of the deceased. So babies and children, and some adults, were inhumed (inside amphoras – often amphoras that had originated not in Greece but in the Levant– if small, in trench graves if larger), while other adults were cremated. The objects deposited with the buried corpses were different from those deposited with the cremated bones: adults who were inhumed received no grave goods, children who were inhumed did receive grave goods; most inhumations in the period 750–700 were accompanied by bronze objects, whereas less than a third of cremations received bronze objects, and inhumations were twice as likely to have oriental scarabs or seals with them, but it was cremations that were most likely to have silver objects accompanying them – two-fifths of all cremations compared to less than a fifth of inhumations (see Table 2.1). These superficially tedious statistics are important because they show that this new community quickly established quite clear general conventions on both how to dispose of its dead and the appropriate way in which to mark their graves, and that those conventions reflected status as well as age.

TABLE 2.1 Pithekoussai grave goods, after Ridgway Table 5

Graves with the following contents	Late Geometric I (c.750–725)		Late Geometric II (c.725–700)	
	Cremations	*Inhumations*	*Cremations*	*Inhumations*
Corinthian pottery	5	4	24	49
Kreis- und Wellenband aryballoi	–	–	10	24
Euboean pottery	2	1	1	5
Argive monochrome	2	3	2	5
Levantine pottery	3	1	1	3
bronze ornaments	7	34	23	91
silver ornaments	9	11	20	17
seals and scarabs	2	22	17	28
Total no. of graves	23	60	50	134

The cultural life of Pithekoussai is illuminated in particular by the pottery. A great deal of the pottery that has been found in the graves takes the form of cups, vessels for mixing wine (kraters), jugs, and other pots associated with drinking parties. Many other pots are small perfume vessels (aryballoi), some made in Corinth, some probably by Phoenicians based in Rhodes, but all of them attesting to the adoption by Greeks of the use of perfumed oil. This was a practice with origins in the Near East, new to the Greek world in the eighth century, and which became closely linked to both the *symposion* and the *gumnasion*. Some of this pottery has figured decoration, and one wine-mixing vessel carries a vivid shipwreck scene with upturned ship and men tipped out among the fish. But the most interesting vessel is a cup, imported from East Aegean and deposited around 720 in a very unusual grave, the cremation of a boy aged about 13. The use of the adult rite for the burial of this boy, along with the number and nature of the other finds in the grave (four kraters, three jugs, several cups, a large number of aryballoi, a silver fibula), suggests that he was of particularly high status. On the cup some lines of verse are scratched, in extremely neat and regular letters whose shapes are characteristic of Euboia and which run from right to left. These verses read: 'I am [*or* 'This is', *or* 'There was'] Nestor's cup good to drink from: whoever drinks from this cup, may desire of fair-garlanded Aphrodite seize him'. It is a remarkable fact that a high proportion of the earliest writing that we have is metrical, and this is not the only example of writing on a pot used at a *symposion* that itself makes reference to the life of the *symposion*. But it is still more remarkable that we should have here a clear reference to epic poetry and the cup of Nestor which figures in *Iliad* 9.632–7:

> a most beautiful cup, which the old man had brought from home, it was studded with rivets of gold and there were four handles to it . . . Another man would strain to move it from the table when it was full, but Nestor, the old man, could lift it with ease.

Most remarkable of all is that the Homeric reference should be a joke: this pottery vessel is not Nestor's cup and is certainly not hard to lift. What is more, the inscription invokes not only epic poetry but also the conventions of the curse – may anyone who does such and such suffer such a fate – but invokes them again in order to subvert them: the fate wished on the drinker here is unlikely to be one that he would regard as undesirable.

In this one grave we see the glittering social life of a community that is at the forefront of all the latest developments. This young man died before he could fully enjoy those urbane witty parties reeking of perfume, at which drinkers showed off the latest technology of communication (the Greek alphabet was probably not more than fifty years old at this point) and alluded knowingly to the hottest of poetic creations – for most scholars now agree that the *Iliad* and *Odyssey* reached the form in which we have them only in the half-century or so *after* this cup was inscribed. Odysseus' tales of his encounter with the Cyclopes who have no law, the man-eating Laestragonian, and the physical dangers of Scylla and Charybdis no doubt reflect one side of Greek voyages into the western Mediterranean in the eighth century, but just as Odysseus' new experiences included the tameable Circe and the pleasures of Calypso's company, so not all the experiences of those who ventured to the west were unpleasant, and the parties at Pithekoussai would shock only an old guard left behind in Greece.

With this picture, built up from material which lay concealed from human knowledge between the end of the eighth century BC and the middle of the twentieth century AD, we can compare what Greeks of the classical and later periods knew of Pithekoussai. In fact Pithekoussai figures only twice in extant ancient literature, on both occasions in writing of the Augustan period. The Roman historian Livy (8.22.5–6), writing at the end of the first century BC, records how Euboeans first landed on Pithekoussai and Aenaria and then moved to the mainland and settled at Cumae. The Greek geographer Strabo, a native of the Black Sea, writing at the same time as Livy, has more detail

(5.4.9): 'Pithekoussai was once inhabited by Eretrians and Chalkidians', he tells us, and goes on to say that the fertility of the land and goldsmithing made them prosperous, but internal dissent, earthquakes and volcanic eruptions caused the island to become deserted. He says that the earlier Sicilian historian Timaius told many wondrous stories about Pithekoussai, but the context in which he does so suggests that those tales were of natural phenomena, not of the inhabitants.

The later abandonment of Pithekoussai no doubt plays some part in accounting for the very thin account that we have of it in later sources. But abandonment of settlements was not at all an uncommon feature of early, or indeed later, Greek history. Several of the archaeological sites whose early Iron Age occupation is best known are well known precisely because they were then abandoned, never reoccupied, and have been available for modern excavation. This is true of the most revealing of all early Iron Age sites in Greece, Lefkandi on Euboea, which has yielded not only rich tombs which show that even in the tenth century BC Greeks remained in contact with the Near East, but also a massive building which suggests sufficient political organisation within the community to command a large labour force, considerable ambition to create a monument on a scale quite unlike contemporary habitations, and building skills of some sophistication. It is also true of Zagora on the Cycladic island of Andros, which has been shown to be a site with regularly planned and close-packed housing, which, when modified, is modified also in a near-uniform fashion. And it is true of a whole slew of other sites in the same geographical region (Koukounaries on Paros, Agios Andreas on Siphnos, Xombourgo on Tenos, Lathouresa in Attica). The abandonment of these sites seems to have had a variety of immediate causes, including warfare, but it is more or less contemporaneous with the settlement by Greeks of sites in Italy and Sicily, and in the north Aegean. Site abandonment and site foundation are both testimony to changing ways of life, the perception of new opportunities, and dissatisfaction with old ways and standards of living.

Classical Greeks themselves had very little knowledge of their early Iron Age history. The settlement of sites abroad was sufficiently momentous for what seem to be largely plausible dates for individual settlements to be accurately preserved down to the fifth century, when Thucydides repeats them as part of his account of how long the Greeks have been in Sicily (Thucydides 6.1–5). As a consequence of this, modern scholars have often assumed that there must be at least a 'kernel' of truth in the stories that classical Greeks told about their past. But to hunt for the kernel is to hunt for an elusive quarry. The stories that arose about the settlement of particular sites were often various. Different ancient authors, for example, ascribe the establishment of a settlement at Metapontum in southern Italy to Nestor, to Achaians on the initiative of neighbouring Sybaris, to a founder named Daulios from Krisa in central Greece, or to a man named Leukippos who 'borrowed' the territory from the Tarentines and then refused to give it back (see Strabo 6.1.15 (C264–5)). It is very unlikely that any of the ancient authors involved simply made up what they reported, rather what their accounts do is reflect, perhaps with some elaboration, stories which those connected with Metapontum in the classical period chose to tell.

Normal scholarly practice has been to dismiss parts of traditions as fabrication and claim other parts as true. In the case of Metapontum, cutting away the fiction starts with Nestor; Nestor cannot be part of history, the argument goes, he is a mythical figure. Such a division between 'myth' and 'history', however, is alien not only to Greek popular storytelling, as we have already seen in the case of stories of athletes, but even to the practice of a historian such as Herodotus. The appearance of Nestor in this tale is typical of the way in which the heroes of Troy, above all Odysseus but also such figures as Nestor, Diomedes, Philoktetes, and, on the Trojan side, Aeneas, came to be associated with places in and around the Adriatic, Italy (including Rome) and Sicily. Those associations are not merely documented in literature but also in the archaeology, as recently with the discovery of rich votive dedications to Diomedes on the island of Palagruza in the

Adriatic. Not only was there no seam for fifth-century Greeks between myth and history, the category of 'myth' in our sense was a creation only of the end of the fifth century. The presence of Nestor in the tradition about the founding of Metapontum almost certainly represents historical reality, the reality that the classical inhabitants of Metapontum linked themselves to the Trojan story through claims of a link with Nestor, a link that may well have been marked in cultic activity.

Uninterested in the truth that Nestor did play a part in Metapontine identity, scholars have generally excised him as an obvious fiction, and then sorted the rest of the traditions recorded in ancient literature according to their judgement of what 'must have been' the case. Judgement of what 'must have been' depends on a general understanding of the whole phenomenon of settlement abroad. The most popular model for later stories was to tell of cities sending out settlers under the command of a 'founder' (*oikistes*) who first consulted the oracle at Delphi on where to found his city. This is indeed more or less the model for new settlements established in the classical period, such as that which the Athenians planned to send, though they may never in fact have sent it, to somewhere called Brea, probably in the northern Aegean, probably c.440 BC We know about this planned settlement from the survival of part of the decree that orders its foundation. In that decree the Athenians make detailed provision for land division, for the setting aside of land for the gods, for the defence of the site, for the future obligations of the settlers with regard to Athens, and for the selection of the settlers (only the less wealthy Athenians are to be eligible). Given, scholars reason, that new settlements established in the fifth century were set up in that way, and given that many stories of earlier settlements talk of the sending out of a founder, surely settlements established in the eighth century must have been just like that?

At the beginning of book 6 of the *Odyssey* we are told how Nausithoos led the Phaiakians away from Hypereia because it was too close to the Cyclopes and set up a new settlement on Scherie, building walls and temples and dividing up the land.

This passage has often been thought to reflect the establishment of new settlements in Italy and Sicily in the late eighth century and so to support the model of a pre-planned settlement established as a political decision by a pre-selected founder. The passage certainly shows that the idea of a centrally organised change of settlement location was perfectly conceivable to the audience who first heard this part of the epic tale. But the circumstances it imagines are not, in fact, the circumstances of most settlements of Greeks abroad: here we have a change of location for a whole community, not the hiving off of a group to found a settlement, leaving the community from which they came still in existence. *Odyssey* 6 is much closer to describing what we might assume to have happened in the late eighth century to the people of Lefkandi, which may have been abandoned because its inhabitants moved to the site of Eretria, or of Zagora, or of any of those abandoned settlements, than to describing a 'mother city' setting up a 'colony'.

When we get a contemporary reference to establishing a settlement abroad in the seventh century, the language which is used is very different from that found in that *Odyssey* passage: 'The scum of all the Greeks ran together to Thasos', writes Archilochos (frg. 102 W). We have to make due allowance for the different genre of Archilochos' poetry, and indeed for his dislike for Thasos, which he described as 'like an ass's back, bristling with wild woods' and as 'not a beautiful place nor a desirable one'(frr. 21, 22 W), but the numbers game alone indicates that normally we must be dealing with settlers drawn from more than one Greek community – no single eighth-century community could have supplied the 5,000–10,000 men to be found at Pithekoussai by 700.

The story of Greek communities taking decisions to establish a settlement of their members across the seas, and selecting founders who will lay out the plan and divide up the land in the new settlement, becomes hard to credit. In the face of the evidence of Archilochos, the heterogeneous material cultures to be found not only at Pithekoussai but at most settlement sites in Sicily and

South Italy, the coexistence of completely different foundation stories, as for Metapontum, and the difficulty of finding enough spare manpower in any single Greek community. There needs to be scope for much more haphazard and opportunist action, for enterprising individuals getting together others from various places, who were discontented in one way or another with their current lot, and were prepared to take the risks, and in some cases the fighting, involved in establishing themselves in another land.

But if we are to recognise that what went on in the eighth and seventh centuries was far less centrally organised than later settlements by Greeks abroad, that means recognising that the language of colonisation, borrowed from Roman veteran settlements and then overlaid with the imperial expansion of European powers from the seventeenth century onwards, is likely to be quite inappropriate, and that what happened in the eighth and seventh centuries BC can only be misleadingly described as 'the age of colonisation'. It also means recognising that the stories told by classical and later writers may be not just contaminated by fictions, they may be systematically fictional.

As we have seen, writing was a new technology for the Greeks in the eighth century, the syllabary used for record keeping in the late Bronze Age, so-called 'Linear B', having been long forgotten. There is much debate on when the Homeric epics got recorded in written form, with some arguing for a sixth-century date, but there is not much doubt that the long hexameter poetry of Hesiod was written down at the point of composition or very soon after, c.700 BC. Poetic texts of all sorts survive from the seventh and sixth centuries and some of these, like those texts of Archilochos about Thasos, allude to past or current events. But the earliest continuous accounts of past events were written in the fifth century, and even in antiquity no earlier prose accounts of past events were available to researchers.

Those earliest prose accounts are critical of the stories handed down by oral transmission. Hekataios of Miletos began his pioneering *Histories* with these words: 'I write what I think is true. In my view the many stories of the Greeks are ridiculous' (frg. 1). He then proceeded to rationalise Greek myths, placing Geryon in Ambrakia in north-west Greece rather than Spain in order to make Heracles' fetching cattle from him credible and turning Cerberus into a snake guarding the entrance to a cave. One of the distinguishing features of Herodotus' histories is his willingness to identify who told the stories that he reports; often he reports different versions of the same events, and in particular cases he makes it explicit that when he repeats a story he does not for that reason imply that he believes it.

The importance of the absence until the fifth century of textual materials on the basis of which to write history lies in the nature of oral traditions. Comparative work in non-literate societies has produced much evidence that when stories are passed down orally, rather than in writing, those who retell the story do so according to their own interests, omitting elements that do not say anything of their current concerns and elaborating other elements to bring out their continuing relevance. This should hardly surprise: selection for a purpose is, after all, exactly what written histories do also, and modern historians similarly introduce new elements into the frame with their 'must have been's.

But the consequences of this are far-reaching for our study of early Greek history. Modern historians have essentially been like Hekataios: they have believed that the 'kernel' of the story handed down in an ancient source must be true, and so they have stripped away elements they consider fantastic and have put the story into a context which they have constructed themselves. But we can have no confidence that there is a kernel of truth in every story: if the interests of those retelling the story over the generations change, then features of the story central to one retelling may be forgotten in the next telling because they are no longer of interest; and features introduced into a telling simply in order to make sense of the central feature may themselves become central to the retelling. Even where a central fact is accurately submitted the framework of interpretation which turns that fact into something of historical interest may have altered radically from one telling to another. Many of the tales told in the fifth century about the distant past may indeed have a kernel of truth, but we can rarely be sure that we can detect that kernel, far less be able to do anything historical with it.

Thucydides, at the beginning of his history, draws attention to the way in which false beliefs can arise very rapidly even about central historical events. 'The mass of the Athenians even believe', he writes, 'that Hipparchos was tyrant when he was killed by Harmodios and Aristogeiton. They do not know that Hippias, because he was the eldest son of Peisistratos, was in charge' (1.20). The issue here is not merely one of getting a family history straight, but of who was responsible for liberating Athens from tyranny and paving the way for democracy. In fact, the killing of Hipparchos in 514 had no effect on tyranny, except to make Hippias act more harshly, and it was the Spartans who liberated Athens in 510, not heroic individual Athenians. Both Herodotus and Thucydides have the 'correct' version of events, but the alternative version was encouraged by the erection of statues of the murderers of Hipparchos, by the public honours passed for them, and by popular songs that hailed their act as bringing constitutional government to Athens. Were it not for written sources – Thucydides himself makes use of a late sixth-century inscription as part of his argument (6.54.7) – we may reasonably doubt whether the 'true' course of events would have survived.

The contemporary pressures which led Athenians to select and elaborate their history in such a way as to falsify the historical record are not hard to find: the Athenians found themselves fighting the Spartans within months of establishing a democratic constitution and continued to be more often hostile than friendly to Sparta throughout the fifth century. Fifth-century Athenians liked to think of themselves as 'sprung from the earth' and as self-sufficient, and their invention of themselves was largely independent of what had actually happened.

In the case of settlements abroad, the pressures that brought about the invention of a history according to what I have called the 'standard model' are only slightly more subtle. The fortunate survival of an inscription from the city of Cyrene in North Africa gives us an exceptionally vivid picture of what happened. Towards the end of the fourth century the people of Thera had something of a crisis, and they attempted to relieve it by making use of their ancestral links with Cyrene. They sent an embassy to Cyrene to 'remind' the people there that at the time that Cyrene had been founded, some 300 years earlier, a sworn agreement had been made according to which a Theran who came to Cyrene at a later date could claim citizenship there. The people of Cyrene bought this story, agreed to grant citizenship to all Therans who settled at Cyrene, and decided to engrave the claimed text of the sworn agreement on a stone and display it. That text duly goes on to stress that the Delphic oracle had spontaneously ordered one Battos and the Therans to found a settlement at Cyrene; that the people of Thera had then made a public agreement that Battos should be leader and king, that Therans should sail as his companions, that those who sailed would be chosen fairly from each family and have equal rights, that if the foundation was successful other Therans could sail later and claim rights, but that if it were not successful, and the Therans could not provide further help, then after five years the settlers might return to Thera and reclaim rights and property there; and so on. It takes little imagination to see how every feature of this sworn agreement could have been used by the Theran ambassadors in the fourth century to establish a moral claim on the people of Cyrene – 'after all, we did undertake that your ancestors could have returned and enjoyed rights in Thera if the settlement wasn't successful'.

In this case we are even better off. For Herodotus also tells the story of the foundation of Cyrene, telling us what was said in the fifth century, a century before the inscription was cut, not only by the people of Thera but also by the people of Cyrene (Herodotus 4.150–6). We can see in the Theran version the general shape of the fourth-century argument: already they are stressing that the settlement was an official and carefully planned expedition. The Cyrenean version, by contrast, lays a lot more stress on Battos, the charismatic leader, who turns out to be the son of a woman persecuted by her stepmother and rescued by the man who is supposed to drown her. The Therans send men to help Battos found a settlement at Cyrene only after disaster has forced them to consult the Delphic oracle, and when the paltry two ships that they send with him fail to make a successful settlement and try to return they drive them off, stoning them.

For the sixth century and much of the fifth century Cyrene was ruled by the Battiad dynasty of kings, for whom Pindar writes victory odes, and the version of their history that the people of Cyrene told clearly reflects the need for a story justifying royal authority. Cyrene was prosperous, partly because of the slightly mysterious 'silphium' plant, and had little reason to look to other cities for help, but Thera, with much more restricted resources, had good reason to want to lay claim to special links with wealthy Cyrene. Cyrene tells the story of the heroic founder who struggled against the odds, Thera the story of the careful planning of a settlement deliberately sent out by public decision. Nor were these the only stories circulating – another told of Cyrene being founded following political strife on Thera.

In so far as a settlement of Greeks was founded at Cyrene and Therans took part in that foundation there is indeed a kernel of truth in these stories. But both stories are highly selective, and the subsequent history of the settlement, as told by Herodotus, along with the nature of the archaeological remains and the more or less contemporaneous settlement by Greeks at other places in Libya, make it very likely that the settlement at Cyrene involved a much more miscellaneous group of Greeks than merely Therans. That there was a particular connection between Thera and Cyrene in the beginning we need not doubt, that the founder of Cyrene came from Thera is highly likely, but that Cyrene was a 'colony' carefully planned by its Theran 'mother city' is surely a product of later wishful thinking.

Where does this leave us in writing the history of early Greece? One reading of what I have been saying would be that we should ditch the literary texts and rely on the archaeology. But this will not in fact do. As those tedious statistics about percentages of different sorts of objects in graves at Pithekoussai showed, archaeology can provide only the thinnest of narratives. The wonderful glimpse of life in late eighth-century BC Pithek-oussai that we get from 'Nestor's Cup' comes, precisely, when we have a text as well as mute objects.

In fact Greek archaeology has very largely been driven by texts. It was the *Iliad* that led Schliemann to Troy, and it has been texts that have dictated both the undertaking of the great majority of major Greek excavations and their interpretation. Surprisingly, perhaps, that is as true of the excavation of Athens as of excavation anywhere else in Greece, and in the case of Athens the guiding text is not even from the classical period, rather it is a text written in the late second century AD by a Greek from Anatolia, Pausanias' *Guide to Greece*. Pausanias' guide-book, with its highly selective description of what there was to see in his day, a description which concentrates on remains of the classical period and earlier and passes over many more recent monuments, has been in the hands of travellers and archaeologists in central and southern Greece ever since the modern 'rediscovery of Greece'. That what we see now when we visit Greek sites is so like what Pausanias saw almost 1,850 years ago is not a matter of chance, for it is according to his description that it has been dug up and restored by archaeologists who have been as keen as Pausanias himself was to remove later accretions to the classical record. When in search of a definition of the Greek polis scholars often quote Pausanias' description of Panopeus in Phokis:

> From Chaironeia you come in 20 stades [4 km] to the polis of Panopeus in Phokis – if a place with no political build-ings, no place for athletics, no theatre, no agora and no fountains, which is perched on the edge of a ravine, can be called a polis. Still the territory has boundary stones with its neighbours, and they send delegates to the Phokian assembly. (10.4.1)

But it is not just because he gives us the most useful checklist of the amenities, institutions and political status that could be expected of a polis that Pausanias can be held to be the inventor of the Greek city as we know it.

Not everything depends on Pausanias. Even from the seventh and sixth centuries there are contemporary texts to guide our interpretation of the archaeology – the poetry of Archilochos or Alkaios, of Tyrtaios and Alkman at Sparta, of Solon at Athens, and so on, but also the epigraphic texts, whether of city laws or of relatively trivial dedications. Nevertheless, more often than not the texts against which we have to read the archaeology of archaic Greece are not contemporary texts but texts that were written, at the earliest, in the fifth century BC. Moses Finley used to snarl despisingly at those who labelled such sources 'primary'. Such sources do not, indeed, so much reflect the history of the cities they discuss as invent it, but our own invention of the early Greek city, for that is what early Greek history is, cannot afford to ignore them.

Chapter 3

How many Greeks were there and how did any of them survive?

Pithekoussai, I suggested in the last chapter, had by the end of the eighth century a population of between 5,000 and 10,000. How big it and other Greek settlements abroad were clearly matters: it matters for the question of whether all who settled at a particular place could have come from a single home city, it matters for the question of the number of ships that will have been required to get them there in the first place, it matters for the question of how much they needed to eat, and whether they could live off the amount of land available to them, it matters for what they could themselves do or produce. We simply cannot understand the position a settlement was in unless we have some idea of how big it was. But how can we tell?

In the case of Pithekoussai, the evidence is archaeological. Four hundred and ninety-three graves dating to the fifty-year period 750–700 have been excavated from what is estimated to be an area between 2.5 and 5 per cent of the whole cemetery in the Valle de San Montano. This suggests that, if the density of burials was constant over the whole cemetery, the total number of burials there was between 9,860 and 19,720. Of these 27 per cent were perinatal deaths; a further 39 per cent were children, up to the age of about 14. These numbers already give some impression of the nature of the community: on average an adult will have been cremated every 5 to 10 days, a baby inhumed once or twice a week, and a child or low-status adult buried between twice a week and every other day. This was a flourishing community in which, as in every ancient community, death was ever present.

To convert the burial numbers to a number for the living population depends upon assuming that all who died received visible burial, and upon knowing the death rate – out of every 1,000 living persons, how many died each year? We have no statistics for death rate in the ancient Greek world, so have to borrow from other societies. The best non-archaeological data from antiquity come from Egyptian census data from the Roman period (dating from between AD 12 and AD 259). Although there are reasons to doubt whether the census is complete and reliable for males, it is plausibly reliable for women. On the basis of it the Egyptian population can be matched up to what is known as a 'Model Life Table', that is a statistical model of the structure of a population with a given life expectancy. The Egyptian data for women seem to fit best with a model known as 'Model West Level 2' in the Princeton Model Life Tables that are standardly used to model pre-industrial populations. This is a model in which life expectancy at birth is taken to be 22.5. Bagnall and Frier suggest that the female death rate in Egypt was between 42 to 49 per thousand, the overall death rate, men and women, 42.1 per thousand (1994: 105).

If that sounds like a high figure, it is. All the evidence from the ancient world suggests that most of those born had a life that was short and unpleasant. For many, including those who were wealthy, what they ate failed to provide them with all the nutrition they needed. 'Deficiency diseases', as they are called, were rife: bladder-stone (caused by too early weaning and insufficient milk), which continued to be endemic in Europe into the nineteenth century (Napoleon suffered from it); rickets (also familiar in the modern world), which is a product of lack of Vitamin D and is well described by the medical writer Soranus; and eye diseases associated with Vitamin A deficiency, for which ancient sources know a genuine cure, eating liver, but recommend also many bogus ones. Analysis of the skeletal material from a classical cemetery in the territory of Metapontum has revealed that 74 per cent suffered from arthritis, that there was a high frequency of a thickening of the skull vault (porotic hyperostosis) associated with anaemia and probably in this case with malaria, and that about 10 per cent of the relevant bones showed signs of periostitis, indicative of systemic infections. There was further evidence that the systemic infection in question was treponematosis, and the distribution of the evidence across skeletons suggests that treponemal infection was a cause of premature death in adults, killing them off in their early 20s; some but not all cases seem to have been of congenital treponematosis, a consequence of venereal disease in the mother. Although teeth showed only moderate dental attrition, suggesting that food was eaten well-cooked, there was a very high incidence of hypoplastic rings, that is rings of thinned enamel that result from periods of disease, malnutrition, or both: in this case the most likely cause was thought once more to be congenital syphilis. There has been considerable scholarly debate about the existence of venereal syphilis in antiquity, but the Metapontum data seem to indicate that both venereal and non-venereal syphilis may be been endemic.

The data from Pithekoussai and those from Egypt that offer a death rate are almost a thousand years apart, and there are many possible reasons why the mortality régime might be different. But adopting, hypothetically, a death rate of 40 per thousand would imply that the mortuary evidence corresponds to a population of between 4,930 and 9,860 for Pithekoussai in the late eighth century. If we divide the graves, as the pottery evidence suggests, between Late Geometric I and Late Geometric II, and assume that the distribution between these periods was the same in the rest of the cemetery as in the excavated portion, we can refine the picture. Between 750 and 725 the population would be between 2,500 and 5,000, and it would grow between 725 and 700 to between 7,360 and 14,720.

How secure are these figures, and what do they mean? It will already have become apparent that to arrive at these figures we have to make a large number of assumptions about the representativeness of the data and about the relationship between death and archaeologically visible burial. There is no way of demonstrating that those assumptions are justified in this case – what we are dealing with is a 'best guess'. But since that best guess is all we can manage, it is worth exploring its various implications.

The first thing to note is that the graves do yield a plausible age structure for the population; that is, although we have no detailed evidence on age at death, the high proportion of infant and child graves is what would be expected in a pre-industrial population. It was only with the so-called 'demographic transition' of the eighteenth and nineteenth centuries in Europe that the chances of a child that was conceived surviving beyond its tenth birthday reached significantly more than 1 in 2. The presence of a large number of child and infant graves is particularly interesting in this case, for it implies that Pithekoussai was not a place of transient residents, serving their time in a 'frontier' area before returning to their native cities to 'settle down'. Rather, these are people who have settled down and have established families.

They may indeed have established their families very successfully. Ironically, the high proportion of infant and child burials may be an indicator of a community that was flourishing, since it is evidence for high fertility. At Pithekoussai not only does the total number of burials almost treble between the third and the last quarter of the eighth century, but the proportion of those burials that are of infants and children also increases. For the population to have trebled in twenty-five years, annual growth of 4 per cent per annum must have been achieved; such a rate is rarely achieved by human populations without some immigration. In this case, if the Egyptian parallel for mortality rate is in the right area, the rate is simply inconceivable without immigration: even to achieve a growth rate of 2 per cent per annum, a population where female life expectancy at birth is 22.5 has to achieve 10 live births for every woman who survived to the end of her reproductive cycle. But if we have to assume that continued immigration contributed to the population growth, the increasing proportion of infants and children, and the fact that they end up accounting for considerably more than half of the burials, suggests that fertility was also high and that although the death rate was also high the birth rate exceeded it.

Who were the new immigrants, and what did a Pithekoussai family consist of? One of the excavators of Pithekoussai, Giorgio Buchner, observed that most safety pins (*fibulae*) found in male graves at Pithekoussai were of Greek type, but *fibulae* found in female graves tended to be of Italian type, even if made on Pithekoussai itself. 'It cannot be supposed', Buchner wrote (1975: 79), 'that the adoption of indigenous personal ornaments was a male idea ... It must have been the women themselves who insisted on wearing native ornaments.' Buchner concluded from that that the women themselves were native. Such a conclusion is premature: there is no reason at all why Greek women on Pithekoussai might not take to Italian types of *fibula* and other ornaments. We do not have to suppose that the initiative came from Greek men for Greek women to be using Italian ornaments. There is, in fact, a lot of evidence from early Greek settlements in Italy and Sicily for the adoption of *fibulae* of Italic types by all sorts of members of the community. What is more, Sicilian and Italian fibula types are one of the most prominent foreign dedications made at the sanctuary of Zeus at Olympia in the late eighth and early seventh centuries. Artefacts travel without the people who made them also accompanying them.

But if we cannot hang the ethnic origin of the women at Pithekoussai on a safety pin, the presence of Italian women in the cosmopolitan community certainly cannot be ruled out. There is, in fact, good reason to think that concern to express a peculiarly Greek identity was in general developed only at the end of the archaic period, and we should not be too quick to assume that moving from an Italic to a predominantly Greek settlement was in any way problematic. There is some quite good evidence for some craftsmen moving between Greek and Etruscan communities, and that Greek settlers on Pithekoussai might have sought wives from the places from which they also acquired metals cannot be ruled out.

Whatever the origin of the women at Pithekoussai, they will not have had an easy life: if their life expectancy was, as in Roman Egypt, between 20 and 25, even a very modest natural growth rate of 0.5 per cent per annum would require, on average, between six and seven live births for every woman who survived to the end of her reproductive cycle. Responsibility was heavy and came quickly: more than a third of children had lost their father by the age of 15 (that is, would have come into their inheritance), and at that age fewer than one in ten will have had a living grandfather.

What are the implications of a population on Pithekoussai that numbered between 7,000 and 14,000 by 700? Let us take consumption first. Adult humans require for survival about 2000 kcals a day, which can be provided by about 600 g wheat a day (220 kg a year). Greeks did not eat bread alone, but cereals were the source of most calories for most people, whether consumed as bread or as porridge. In some parts of Greece, at least, barley was grown rather than wheat because it was more drought-resistant and therefore less prone to failure. When wheat was grown it was durum wheat, the wheat from which pasta is now made, and which is less suitable for bread; bread wheat did not grow well in Greece but did grow in the Black Sea, from which it began to be exported in quantity perhaps only in the sixth century. The cereal-heavy diet was supplemented with olive oil and wine. Olive oil was already being exported from Attica by 700 BC in a characteristic form of amphora, the so-called SOS amphora, all over the Mediterranean: SOS amphoras were both imported to and imitated on Pithekoussai. Meat was consumed primarily in connection with religious festivals. In classical Athens such festivals were frequent, and some Athenians at least would eat sacrificial meat several times a week, but we have no evidence for the levels of religious activity or meat consumption in Pithekoussai.

Even allowing for the relatively high proportion of infants and children, the population of Pithekoussai in 700 will have needed the equivalent of between 880,000 and 1,760,000 kg of wheat a year. There is some direct evidence for agricultural production in Greek antiquity, but it is hard to use, partly because the area from which it was produced is not accurately known, partly because the high degree of variation in production from year to year means that a single year's figures may be highly misleading. Comparative evidence has been variously interpreted by scholars, with pessimistic estimates suggesting yields of only c.500 kg per ha., a fifth of which would be needed for seed, and optimistic estimates up to three times that amount. The probable existence of biennial fallow, with at best a fodder crop grown in the alternate year, further complicates calculations. Olive trees, which have a heavy crop only every other year, seem on average to produce approximately the same number of calories per hectare as do cereals.

Even on relatively generous assumptions about productivity, a family of five seems to have needed about 3 ha. of land to support them, whether they cropped that land with cereals alone, cereals and olives, or whatever. Recent calculations suggest that on Pithekoussai between 1,000 and 2,000 ha. were cultivable. If we take the higher of these figures, and suppose that by 700 all cultivable land was indeed cultivated, then 3,333 of the population of Pithekoussai could be fed from food grown on the island, that is in rough terms between half and a quarter of the actual population. If we take the lower figure then clearly we are dealing with between an eighth and a quarter of the population. For the rest, food would need to be imported – perhaps 440,000 kg of wheat, perhaps three times that amount. Four hundred and forty tons means about four dedicated shiploads of grain with ships of 100 tons or so, as seems most likely for this period. That, or even the twelve ships that the larger population would require, may not seem very much, but with a shipping season that is only six months long the willingness to rely on imported grain to this degree implies a high degree of confidence in the regularity of shipping.

45

These issues of consumption can also be looked at the other way round, as issues of production. The equivalent of at least 600 to 1,300 families will have supported themselves by non-agricultural activities. In a significant number of cases this activity will have involved ships and exchange, but the archaeological evidence suggests that craft activity also had a part to play. We have to imagine a community with a relatively complex division of labour where a large part of the population lived by trade and craft activity, not by subsistence farming.

Pithekoussai was certainly not a typical Greek city in many respects, but just how atypical was it? Even on the issue of size, it is extremely hard to answer this question. Frustratingly, we possess similarly rich cemetery data from very few other Greek communities, and there is no case where we can make even the sort of educated guess at the total number of people buried in a given period that we can make at Pithekoussai. But we know enough about other places to be sure that they were different. Take Athens, for example, in the same period. There too large numbers of graves have been excavated, and there too scholars have attempted to deduce facts about the population from the numbers of graves. In this case the deductions concern not the total number of people, but the way in which the population changed over time, on the assumption that the numbers of burials known from different periods is in a more or less constant relationship to the number of burials that occurred in those periods. Unfortunately the Athenian grave evidence differs markedly from that at Pithekoussai in one crucial respect: at Pithekoussai infant and child burials are well represented; in Athens down to the second quarter of the middle of the eighth century, and again from soon after 700, the number of child graves is only a very small proportion of the number of adult graves. This is demographically simply impossible. Athenians must during those periods have disposed of dead babies and children in some way that is impossible to recover archaeologically, and we cannot be sure that they did not dispose similarly of some adults also.

This is an important reminder that what archaeology finds is not a random but a skewed sample of what once existed. As we have already seen at Pithekoussai, communities distinguish between their members by the way in which they bury them, making burial a means of recognising or indeed ascribing status. At Athens archaeologically visible burial, for all but the period c.750–680, seems to have been given only to people of a certain status. That for those seventy years things were different raises questions which archaeologists and historians need to answer, but it deprives us of the possibility of using the burial record to calculate the changing size of the population.

From the classical period we have epigraphic and literary data from which we can attempt to reconstruct population sizes. Although literary sources occasionally offer figures for the total population of a city, these are rarely trustworthy. A character in Menander argues that the gods cannot possibly concern themselves with whether every individual is up to good or bad, given that there are 1,000 cities and each of them has 30,000 inhabitants (*Epitrepontes* 1084–91). Our best evidence comes from army figures, and the best of all from Thucydides on Athenian resources in 432 (Thucydides 2.13.6–8). Although Thucydides' figures are not without their problems, they indicate a fifth-century Athenian adult male citizen population of about 50,000, which suggests that taking men, women, and children together there were around 200,000 Athenians, not counting slaves or resident foreigners. Total population numbers are likely to have been in the region of 300,000.

The size of Athens was quite exceptional among Greek cities, but it went with a very large territory, and the walled area of the town of Athens itself probably housed less than a quarter of the population. The territory of Attica covered some 240,000 ha., giving a population density of about 1.25 people per ha. in the fifth century. This is actually lower than the population density for Pithekoussai, which works out at between 1.5 and 3 persons for each of the 4,640 ha. of the island. But it compares with an estimated population density of Italy during the early empire of between 0.26 and 0.29 persons per ha. In the fourth century the Athenian adult male population dropped to around 30,000 and the total number of inhabitants of Attica to something closer to 200,000.

Menander's estimate that there were 1,000 Greek cities was an under-estimate rather than an over-estimate – the very large number of communities enjoying some sort of political self-determination is one of the characterising features of classical Greece. But if Athens vastly exceeded Menander's 30,000 inhabitants in size, many other cities did not even approach that figure. Epigraphic evidence enables us to make an informed guess at the population of Koressia, one of four cities on the island of Keos, and suggests that we may be dealing with something in the order of 800–1,300 people, 150–260 adult male citizens. But then the territory of Koressia amounts to some 1,500 ha. only, much of which is not cultivable except when terraced (and the extent of terracing in antiquity cannot now be determined).

The population of Greece in the fifth and fourth centuries was certainly significantly greater than in the eighth century, but even among classical cities Pithekoussai would have ranked as middling in absolute size, with plenty of smaller as well as plenty of larger cities, but unusual in population density. In 700 it was probably the most densely occupied Greek settlement as well as one of the largest Greek communities. But what about its economic base? Was its heavy engagement in trade and reliance on imported food exceptional, or a pattern widely repeated?

The data which we used to deduce the high degree to which Pithekoussai relied on imported food, and therefore the extent to which it was implicated in exchange networks, were its population and its agricultural capacity. Not only is Pithekoussai unique among eighth-century Greek settlements in giving us reasonably good evidence for population, but the fact that it is a small island enables much more confident measurement of agricultural capacity than would normally be the case. The sorts of calculation entered into above simply cannot be done for other cities. For Athens and its territory, for instance, there are modern figures for the cultivated area, but there is also clear evidence of terracing systems indicative of past cultivation of significantly larger areas. Terraces are hard to date, however, and although the chances are that the systems go back to antiquity, there are also some indications that at least some of the terraces were in use for only a short time. The potential error in any guess about how much of Attica was under cultivation is enormous. And much the same applies elsewhere.

So how do we deduce how Greek communities of the archaic and classical periods supported themselves? Hardly anything survives in classical literature which would count as self-conscious economic analysis. The closest we come to that is a work by Xenophon entitled *Poroi*, often translated as *Ways and Means*. In that work Xenophon considers the resources of Athens and how Athens could improve its economic position. The work has four chapters. The first praises the natural advantages of Athens in terms of its fertility (not all ancient writers agreed!) and position. The second chapter proposes that prosperity would increase if the Athenians attracted more non-Athenian residents: non-Athenians resident in Athens on a permanent basis paid taxes to Athens, including a poll tax (the *metoikion*), but had no political rights; they could not own land and so were primarily involved in craft activity and exchange. Famous metics included the father of Lysias, who owned a shield factory during the Peloponnesian War, and employed 120 slaves working in it. Xenophon proposes that Athens should reduce the burdens on metics by relieving them of military service and improving their conditions by allowing them to buy houses. In the third chapter he considers ways to make Athens better for merchants, so as to increase the amount of imports and exports and so of the taxes that went with them. In the fourth chapter he advocates increasing mining activity in the silver mines of Laureion by the state purchasing slaves and hiring them out. Throughout the work, what we would call economic analysis is infrequent and jejune. Although aware of supply and demand enough to claim that silver alone is free of its rules, Xenophon operates in general as if marginal changes to the institutional framework of social relations in the city will have significant effects upon patterns of economic activity – as if it was the threat that they might have to do military service that kept non-Athenians from moving to Athens, the inefficiencies of the courts that dissuaded merchants from sailing to Athens, or the need to hire slaves from private owners that prevented people taking up options in the silver mines. All of these particular claims are implausible, and it is not surprising that Xenophon's pamphlet appears to have had little or no effect, but recent work in modern economic history has stressed the importance of institutional factors, and Xenophon's basic approach to understanding the economy deserves a more sympathetic treatment than scholars have yet given it.

The impression given by the *Ways and Means* of an amateur observer offering superficial answers to economic questions is somewhat reinforced by two works entitled *Oikonomikos* or *Oikonomika*. *Oikonomikos* is the title of another short work by Xenophon, this time a Socratic dialogue in which Socrates discusses household management with one Ischomachos. We have met this work once already, when looking for evidence on the age of marriage. The *Oikonomikos* is indeed a very useful source of evidence for the sorts of behaviour an Athenian took for granted – whether this is behaviour towards women or behaviour towards slaves. It is very much less useful, however, either as evidence for what actually occurred (what we have is prescription not description, and the prescriptions of a man of wealth) or as evidence about the economy. Xenophon is far more concerned to argue for the virtues of farming as the proper training for citizens than he is to analyse the economics of agriculture. The rather different *Oikonomika*, preserved among the works of Aristotle, does have some more theoretical discussion of economics, at a general level, but its second book is full of financial stratagems, clever tricks by which cities and their rulers have raised revenues, rather than any discussion of what we would call economics. But just as the existence of ancient collections of clever military tricks, such as Polyainos' *Strategemata*, does not show that no one in antiquity thought about the overall shape of military campaigns, so the triviality of Book II of the *Oikonomika* says nothing about how the economy worked in fact and does not show that no one did understand, or could have understood, either their personal or their city's economy.

Was the failure of the Greeks or the Romans to develop economics as a subject of inquiry simply a matter of intellectual shortcoming or was it a product of the nature of the ancient economy? That it was the latter was the main contention of M.I. Finley, whose *Ancient Economy* is really about how the Greeks and Romans did not have an economy in the modern sense: 'There were no business cycles in antiquity; no cities whose growth can be ascribed . . . to the establishment of a manufacture; no "Treasure by Foreign Trade"' (1973a: 23). The Greek and Roman world was not, Finley insisted, 'an enormous conglomeration of interdependent markets'; rather it was a matter of subsistence economies and minimal division of labour.

What Finley is prepared to take as evidence determines his conclusions. For all his contempt for the 'crashing banality' (p. 20) of the Aristotelian *Oikonomika* and his acknowledgement that Xenophon's *Oikonomikos* 'is fundamentally a work of ethics' (p. 18), it is writers such as Xenophon and Cicero who provide him with most of the evidence he discusses. By contrast, the evidence on which the picture of Pithekoussai around 700 which I offered above is built comes from archaeology, from comparative demography, from comparative studies of Mediterranean agriculture, and from what we know of basic human nutritional requirements. Unless the deductions which are made by extrapolation from a small archaeological sample are seriously misleading, and they may be, we can be absolutely confident that Pithekoussai in 700 was not dominated by subsistence farmers.

Not every settlement in 700, clearly, was a Pithekoussai, but could Pithekoussai have been alone in this respect? To this question, I want to argue, the answer must surely be 'no'. The demand for imported food generated by Pithekoussai was in aggregate very modest. Such demand cannot itself have generated the sort of infrastructure of shipping upon which it relied. Anyone shipping grain in the direction of Pithekoussai needed to be sure that if someone else had got there first they would still be able to find an alternative market for their cargo. It used to be held that, since practically anywhere in the Mediterranean can grow grain and vines, and since most of the low-altitude parts of the Mediterranean can also grow olives, these staples were moved around only when crop failure hit a particular region. Increasing knowledge of the distribution of amphoras, whose shape indicates their origin, has revealed that these containers in which oil and wine were shipped travelled widely and in all directions, in patterns not plausibly explained by periodic crop failure. This has further encouraged attention to be paid to ancient texts which proudly catalogue available luxuries: one of the best pieces of evidence being chapter 27 of the Old Testament book of the Prophet Ezekiel, written in the seventh and sixth centuries, which talks of purple, blue and red saddle-cloths from Cyprus and Ionia, and of bronze, slaves, iron cassia, ivory and ebony from Rhodes (not the ultimate origin of any of these items, of course).

The problem which we face is converting the textual references and archaeological finds into some sort of quantitative assessment. Finley was right to insist that catalogues of items imported or exported are useless unless we can establish quantities and ratios, but by doing so he also guaranteed that his own position was unassailable: some commodities are archaeologically visible, some are not; some commodities are such as to attract the attention of writers of poetry, others not. Only a complete list of ships' cargoes over a whole year would bring us at all close to being able to quantify the movement of goods. In fact the best we can do is probably the description of the cargo of a single vessel sailing out of Athens in the fourth century. This description occurs because of a subsequent court case over the liabilities arising from the sinking of the ship. As part of this case the contract entered into by the shipowner was read out in court ([Demosthenes] 35.10–13) and compared with what the ship in fact, it was alleged, did. The contract specified that 3,000 jars of

Mendean wine were to be carried from Mende or Skione to the Black Sea, but the story is that they put on only 450 jars of wine, and that before the ship foundered these were sold and all the ship was carrying between Pantikapeion and Theodosia on the north littoral of the Black Sea was 80 jars of Koan wine, put on at Pantikapeion for a farmer from Theodosia for his workers, plus a jar or two of wool, eleven or twelve jars of dried fish, and two or three bundles or goat skins. The prosecution wants the court to believe that the sinking was a set-up job, designed so that the shipowners would not have to pay back the money they had borrowed. The story is designed, therefore, to emphasise the oddities of the practice involved. But if we believe the version which the court is told, then the transport of large quantities of wine from the north Aegean to the Black Sea was regular. Although, as is explicitly stated at [Demosthenes] 35.35, only certain wines (from Mende, Thasos, Peparethos and Kos) got transported around the place (labels mattered), items like wine were sold on, not merely taken from place A to place B to be consumed at place B, and it would be relatively unusual for a vessel to sail around without a full cargo.

The details in the contract and witness statements argue in favour of seeing the pattern of exchange that lies behind this court case as typical. The loan that is at issue was advanced jointly by an Athenian, Androkles from the deme of Sphettos, and Nausikrates from the Euboean city of Karystos. The people who took the loan were two men from the city of Phaselis in southern Asia Minor. The witnesses to the contract include a banker from the Piraeus, a Boeotian and an Athenian. Witness statements to the effect that only 450 jars of Mendean wine were put on board and concerning what was on board at the time of the shipwreck were given by a man from Halikarnassos who travelled as supercargo. Another man from Halikarnassos claims to have made a further loan on the cargo, and yet a third man from Halikarnassos bears witness to a third loan, this time advanced by a man from Kition in Cyprus to the captain of the ship. How are we to explain this cosmopolitan group? It is perhaps compatible with two opposing views: that shipping was so infrequent that money to finance it had to be gathered from any and every available quarter; and that shipping was on such a large scale that individuals could and did find themselves able to circulate their money as they themselves circulated. One further observation makes only the latter view tenable: these loans are being pursued in the courts. The mechanism of credit is clearly well backed up with legal support. Even across city jurisdictions lenders of money can expect to pursue debtors in the courts. We have evidence for such agreements well before the date of this speech – as it happens one of the best-preserved early agreements is between Athens and Phaselis (ML 31). We have already seen that Xenophon thinks facilitating court actions important to facilitating trade, and that the Aristotelian *Oikonomika* imagines a world in which at any particular time a large number of people in a city will have grievances with and claims on ships of other cities. All of this argues for the large-scale movement of goods between cities being important from an early date. Indeed early enough, we might suggest, to secure the supplies needed to keep alive the community at Pithekoussai in 700.

Chapter 4

Law, tyranny and the invention of politics

Consideration of the extent of exchange in the archaic and classical Greek world plunges us rapidly into issues of law. Some kind of mechanism for dispute settlement has to exist in any community, as it exists in any family. The *agon* that is the court-case goes back in Greek literature just as far as the *agon* that is the athletic competition. Dispute settlement lies at the heart of both Homeric epics: the *Iliad* turns on the difficulty of finding a satisfactory settlement to the dispute between Achilles and Agamemnon, and what happens in the end is less that a solution is found than that the parties come to view matters differently. The *Odyssey* relies on the suitors' inability to settle the question of which of them is to get Penelope's hand, and upon a criterion for dispute settlement, the ability to draw the bow, which none of them can manage. In Hesiod's *Works and Days* it is part of the one-sided settlement of the dispute between Zeus and Prometheus that determines the human condition and the fact that men have to labour to produce food. What is more, both the *Iliad* and *Works and Days* allude to more mundane dispute settlement in the world with which their audience could be expected to be familiar.

On the shield which Hephaestus makes for Achilles the scene of the city at peace includes a gathering of the people in the agora to watch the elders offer judgement on a dispute over whether or not a man who has killed another should be allowed to buy himself off (*Iliad* 18.497–508). The elders are apparently to offer their individual judgements, the case is decided according to the 'straightest judgement', and the 'straightest' judge takes home two talents of gold. Straightness of judgement is at issue too in Hesiod's *Works and Days* where Hesiod complains that his brother Perses has taken more than his share of their inheritance, then argued his case before the *basileis* ('kings') and, apparently, won it (*Works and Days* 27–41). Hesiod implies that the victory was achieved by bribes, thereby perhaps explaining the enormous sum offered for straight judgement on the shield of Achilles: one can ensure one gets good judgements only by making straight judgement more financially worthwhile than crooked judgement.

Although some translations introduce it, law is not at issue in either the *Iliad* or *Works and Days*. The principles which the elders in the one case and the *basileis* in the other are expected to operate are principles of fairness. The same sort of procedure was held by Aristotle to operate still in classical Sparta (*Politics* 2, 1270b28–31); Aristotle is critical of the fact that the ephors, who did not have to have any special qualification for that most important elected office, decided cases on the basis of their own judgement and not according to written laws. But, as Aristotle's contrast implies, by the classical period the expectation was that law would be written.

The earliest written laws to survive date from the seventh century. We might expect them to concern precisely those matters that are at issue in the disputes in the *Iliad* and *Works and Days* – that is, crimes against the person and crimes against property. But in fact the constant focus of early laws is not on homicide, theft or other such matters of substance, rather they reflect that other feature of the disputes in Homer and Hesiod – an obsession with procedure.

The closest link with the dispute on the shield of Achilles is found in the one provision that survives in detail from the laws for which Drako was responsible at Athens in the late seventh century. This provision survives because it continued to be current Athenian law and was reinscribed as part of the writing up of the Athenian laws at the end of the fifth century. This law does, precisely, concern homicide and the circumstances in which someone guilty of accidental killing can be pardoned, but it elaborates not upon the circumstances in which a killing can be held to be accidental ('unintentional' in the Greek formulation) but upon the conditions which have to apply with regard to the family of the victim for pardon to be granted.

Drako's homicide law has a place in the story of how vendetta was ended and dispute settlement taken over by the city. Other surviving early laws, however, display much more concern at the growing power of the state than at the surviving powers of the family. So a seventh-century law from Dreros on Crete provides that the chief magistracy should only last a year and should not be held by the same individual more than once in ten years. A law of about the same date from Tiryns in the Argolid testifies to a great hierarchy of magistrates who are required to check up on each other and are subject to the overall scrutiny of the whole community and of a magistrate who has powers even over the community. A law from early sixth-century Chios seems similarly to show the regulation of magistracies and the ultimate jurisdiction of a popular council upon which each of the tribes of the people is represented equally and by a large number of representatives (fifty).

We find a rather similar body of concerns in what is known as the Spartan *rhetra*, a law preserved in Plutarch's life of the legendary Spartan lawgiver Lykourgos, and almost certainly derived by Plutarch from the *Constitution of the Lakedaimonians* produced by Aristotle's research team in the third quarter of the fourth century. The antiquity of this law seems to be guaranteed not simply by the obscurity of some of its language, which required Aristotelian exposition, but by the way in which a poem by the Spartan seventh-century poet Tyrtaios seems to refer to it. The law provides for regular meetings of an assembly and for that assembly to be sovereign; whether Plutarch's claim that the rider allowing 'crooked decisions' to be overridden by the Council of Elders was a later addition has been debated by scholars.

These laws, which come from widely scattered Greek cities and were moved at various times in the century and a half after 700, reveal the widespread development of complex magisterial structures, along with a consistent concern both to police the magistrates' execution of their obligations and to ensure that they do not arrogate to themselves powers that the community wished to belong to itself. There are no signs in any of these laws of a battle between the people and an aristocracy, but there are plenty of signs of mutual suspicion within a group, many or all of whom are eligible for magisterial office. There is also clear concern that ultimate responsibility should rest either with the whole body of (ex-)magistrates or with the whole community (though we cannot know who were included or excluded by terms such as 'people' (*demos*) or 'mob' (*okhlos*)).

In terms of the history of law, the consistent concern of early Greek laws with procedure does not fit into a neat developmental picture in which dispute settlement is wrested from the family by the state. Nor does it fit into a picture of legal energies being devoted to producing laws that, while not ceasing to be general rules, take adequate account of particular circumstances. For all that Euripides, in his tragedy *Suppliant Women* (433–4), could have Theseus claim that 'when the laws have been written down both the weak and the rich have equal justice', even Aristotle (*Politics* 1287b4–8) was prepared to admit that the judgement of an individual magistrate could be more secure than action according to written law. The piling up of qualification upon qualification, which is to be glimpsed in the extraordinary series of magistrates watching over one another in the Tiryns law, is found more generally in much Greek law. One example, which became classic even in antiquity, was a law attributed to Solon at Athens which laid down that a will was valid provided that, at the time of writing it, the testator was not senile, drunk, drugged, in chains or under the influence of a woman. Far from ensuring equality, what such a law did was to put power into the hands of the magistrate or court hearing the case, as exactly what counted as senile or influence, or whatever, was weighed up.

The story that the obsession of early law with procedure does fit into is the story of politics. The city of Achilles' shield has its elders, the city of Perses and Hesiod its *basileis*, who must be not 'kings' but magistrates, even if they are perhaps to be thought of as hereditary. Later Greek traditions offer little information on how communities were governed in this period, and Greeks themselves largely guessed about early forms of government by reckoning that some of the constitutions that they observed around them were older (because 'more primitive') than others. So, some ancient political theorists suggested that Greek cities tended to enjoy a sequence that began with kings and passed into hereditary aristocracy, and that the aristocracy was then succeeded by tyrants who championed the people before being overthrown by them as they established democracy.

This evolutionary model, like most such models, fits some of the facts. From the middle of the seventh century individuals who usurp powers and set themselves up as the final arbiters appear in a large number of Greek cities. These men came to be known as 'tyrants', and far from replacing existing constitutional arrangements they appear often to have left them to operate, reserving the right to override all decisions made elsewhere. The word 'tyrant' was probably borrowed from the east, which suggests that the idea of despotic rule by a single man was one with which the Greeks first became familiar there. So it is that Archilochos, again, in the first surviving use of the word in the middle of the seventh century, denies, in the same breath, that he envies the wealth of Gyges and that he wants tyranny. Gyges' story opens Herodotus' *Histories* since it is with Gyges' murder of Kandaules and assumption of power in Lydia that, as Herodotus understands it, the sequence of events begins that leads to the conquest of Lydia by Persia and so to the direct encounter between

Persians and Greeks that Herodotus sets out to chart. Herodotus' story of Gyges also establishes another motif recurrent in Greek accounts of tyranny, and indeed of monarchy more generally: a link with improper behaviour towards women.

The earliest tyranny about which any detailed tradition survived in the fifth century was that of Kypselos in Corinth. Corinth, the story went, had been previously in the hands of the family of the Bacchiadai, who held on to power in an increasingly exclusive fashion. According to Herodotus (5.92) Kypselos was the son of a woman who was a Bacchiad by birth but because lame could find no Bacchiad husband and so married outside the family. An attempt by the Bacchiads to murder her offspring was foiled (the baby smiled), and when he grew up he seized power. Typically, another tradition held, incompatibly, that Kypselos became a magistrate at Corinth and earned a good reputation for his fair judgements, and that on the basis of this he seized power – acting exactly in the way that the Dreros law seeks to prevent.

Herodotus puts the story of Kypselos into the mouth of a Corinthian, named Sosikles or Sokles, who tells it in order to warn the Spartans and their allies off reinstalling Hippias as tyrant of Athens. Whether or not the tradition that a Corinthian told this story on this occasion was an accurate one, most tyranny stories seem to have been handed down by people who belonged to cities which had freed themselves of tyranny, and were told as cautionary tales in a world where the danger of an individual setting himself up in power continued to be a real one. It is not very surprising that the last thing Sokles says about Kypselos is: 'Once he had become tyrant, Kypselos became the sort of man who chased many out of Corinth, deprived many of their property, and most, by some way, of their lives.' That same motif occurs in a story that gets into histories of Rome that one of the Bacchiadai, Demaratos, who got involved in trade with Etruria, decided to translate himself entirely to Italy when Kypselos took power.

As Sokles goes on the story gets worse. Kypselos is succeeded by his son Periander, who starts off milder but on the advice of another tyrant, Thrasyboulos of Miletos, that the tallest ears of grain should be lopped off, he turns nasty, finishing off those Corinthians left alive by his father. His nastiness is then demonstrated by a story of how he stripped the women of Corinth of their finery, all in order to discover the location of some buried treasure from his dead wife, whom he consulted via the oracle of the dead. There is virtually nothing here other than one folk-tale motif after another.

Stories that clearly come out of the same stable as those about Periander were told also about other tyrants of this period. Myron tyrant of Sikyon is said to have been 'uncontrolled in other respects and particularly in his relations with women. He raped them not only secretly but openly. In the end he had an adulterous affair with the wife of his brother Isodemos.' Peisistratos became tyrant of Athens, according to tradition, on three occasions. On the second occasion he did so after having made a deal with a political rival, Megakles, involving Peisistratos marrying Megakles' daughter. But the coalition collapsed after his new wife revealed to her mother, in a charming vignette in Herodotus' account (1.61), that her husband was having sex with her 'not in the conventional way'.

Periander appears elsewhere in ancient literature as one of the seven wise men and an author of verse. Peisistratos' tyranny, which in Herodotus' account is full of tricks and guile, is presented elsewhere as having been a 'golden age', 'the reign of Kronos'. These men and other tyrants were figures whose life stories it was attractive to improve in the telling. They came to stand for the idea of tyranny, and it was important that they did so since that idea had continued currency, and not simply as an idea. The major cities of Sicily, for instance, all of which were reputed to have had tyrants in the sixth century, were only rid of them for a short while in the fifth century before Dionysios of Syracuse and others claimed power for themselves in the late fifth and fourth centuries. Tyrants crop up in cities large and small throughout our narrative histories of the fifth and fourth centuries. So we meet the well-named Euarchos, tyrant of Astakos in north-west Greece, thrown out of his city by Athenian military intervention at the beginning of the Peloponnesian War and then running off to Corinth to get the Corinthians to restore him (Thucydides 2.30.1, 2.33.1). Or we meet Euphron, the opportunist politician at Sikyon in the north-east Peloponnese in the early fourth century, who plays the various larger powers operating in the area off against one another and sets himself up as tyrant, only to be assassinated (Xenophon *Hellenica* 7.1–3). Or we meet Jason of Pherai in Thessaly, a man who almost brings off a political unification to turn Thessaly into a major military power in the third decade of the fourth century; he could present himself as legally appointed to his position, but when he is assassinated the rest of the Greek world treat his assassins as heroic tyrannicides (Xenophon *Hellenica* 6.1, 6.4.20–32).

That we can put no trust in any of the details that we find in the later accounts of them, does not mean that tyranny was not a real phenomenon in archaic Greece. But it does mean that we have to be very careful about the basis on which we explain the phenomenon, and about the ways in which ancient analysts explained it. The most influential of the ancient analysts is Aristotle. Aristotle offers several accounts of the circumstances in which tyranny came about in Greek cities; he puts most emphasis on tyrants coming to power on the back of popular support, either directly to replace earlier kings or to replace oligarchies, but he admits that some of the stories told about archaic Greek cities suggested that tyranny could arise directly from oligarchy or even kingship (*Politics* 1310b7–31). What Aristotle is doing in his analysis in *Politics* is clear: he is thinking through the traditions about Greek tyrants of which he is aware and considering how well they fit into any particular pattern. In doing this he is doing exactly the same exercise that modern scholars do, though the fund of traditions upon which he draws may be richer.

Aristotle makes one suggestion which modern scholars have taken up with particular enthusiasm: that there might be a link between tyranny and the arming of the citizen body (*Politics* 1297b16–24, 1305a17–36). The reason for suggesting that something dramatic happened to the way in which Greek cities fought wars comes from comparison of descriptions of warfare in the *Iliad* with descriptions of warfare in classical texts. In the *Iliad* the emphasis is upon the individual warrior, who gets driven to battle in a chariot, and appears to fight surrounded by a great deal of space; Homeric warriors have opportunities to enter into conversation, and even to exchange armour, on the battlefield. Chariots make no appearance in classical battle descriptions and, the battles of Alexander the Great excepted, individual warriors are but rarely referred to; everything is about what the right wing or left wing of the army achieves, about breaking up the enemy line, not about securing individual scalps.

Is the difference between Homeric and classical battle descriptions merely a literary matter, with a work interested in individuals concentrating on individuals, and works interested in the fates of whole cities concentrating on the battle line as a whole? Or was there a substantial change in the nature of warfare? Two technical differences between Homeric and classical warfare are certain: Homeric warriors throw spears, classical warriors do not, they thrust with them; and Homeric shields seem to be suspended on straps round the neck while classical shields are held by an arm strap. These two features go together: the shield held firmly on the left arm made sense only in close ranks, where the warrior's right side could be protected by the shield of his right-hand neighbour, and throwing spears was neither convenient for a warrior in close formation nor likely to be effective against heavily armed massed ranks. Putting all this together, many scholars have concluded that at some point old styles of loosely ordered battle between heroic champions were succeeded by closely packed battle lines that engaged each other in something closer to a rugby scrum.

Any replacement of warfare between champions by warfare by massed infantry could be expected to have social and political repercussions. If the safety of the city ceases to depend upon the few and comes to depend upon the many, then it is to be predicted that the many who defend the city will come to expect some sort of say in how cities are run. Once more men of the city are armed, there is more chance of a single charismatic leader exploiting their discontent in order to put himself in charge. Changes in warfare, in this story, enabled tyranny, and stories of tyrants with bodyguards, and of men who held the office of pole-march (lit. 'leader in war') becoming tyrant, are taken as support for this sequence of events.

Unfortunately, the evidence that we have does not give much support to these stories. Close reading of the *Iliad* shows that massed ranks already exist in that poem: the focus may be on Patroklos and Achilles, but the Myrmidons are there raising the dust in the background. Numbers do matter, even in Homeric epic. What is more, the *Iliad* describes the arming of warriors in elaborate detail, and their armour is heavy armour, ill-suited to racing around Troy in and, except in the details of the shield, actually close to the armour which is held to have condemned the classical warrior to fight in close ranks. The shield, which has been considered to be crucial, makes its appearance in Greek art in the first half of the seventh century, with a scene, which was never bettered in Greek art, of two armies advancing against each other, kept in time by a piper. That such a shield was unknown before the seventh century is primarily a contention derived from archaeological silence, but, regardless of the date of the first hoplite shield, the invention of a shield which can only be used effectively in massed ranks presupposes that massed ranks already exist. The moment at which warfare in massed ranks replaced warfare of individual champions would have to be put in the eighth century, significantly before the appearance of the earliest tyrants in Greek tradition.

Most recently, even the belief that the hoplite shield demanded that warriors form up shoulder to shoulder for their own protection has been questioned. Hans van Wees has pointed out that to maximise thrust the warrior does not want to present a flat chest to the enemy, but to present his left shoulder to the enemy, enabling the sideways body to make full advantage of the stretch of the legs, as with the javelin thrower. But if it is only the left side that is facing the enemy, the shield that is fixed to the left arm is in precisely the right place to offer full protection, and the shelter provided by the shield of a neighbour in the ranks is not required. Hoplite lines could therefore be less than completely closely packed, and the reason for packing closely was not protection but to prevent the enemy from breaking through and attacking from behind.

As a key to the development of tyranny, the invention of the hoplite shield needs to be laid aside: it probably happened too early, and it probably made very little difference to the nature of warfare. But if changing modes of warfare were not a crucial factor, can we point to any period-specific reasons for tyranny as a political development?

Our best evidence for the political pressures that arose in the archaic Greek city and the way in which those made tyranny possible comes from Athens, and it concerns not the man who did become tyrant there, Peisistratos, but the man who insists that he did not, Solon. Solon is another who figures among the Seven Wise Men, and he quickly attracted stories whose historicity is extremely dubious. So in the first book of his histories (1.29–33) Herodotus tells of a meeting between Solon and the fabulously rich king of Lydia, Kroisos, in which Kroisos wants to be told that he is the happiest man in the world, only for Solon to insist that the happiest man was an obscure Athenian named Tellos who fathered sons who had children of their own and then died fighting, at something over the age of sixty evidently, for his country. Chronologically a meeting between Solon and Kroisos is hard to square with known dates, and the story told has nothing plausible about it. But if the nice things later recorded about Solon are no more credible than the nasty things later recorded about Periander, we have the advantage with Solon that his own writings have survived.

Solon wrote poetry. Some of that poetry has no bearing on historical events. There are lines which discuss man's life in terms of a succession of ten seven-year periods (frg. 27 W, a sort of up-market version of the tale of Solomon Grundy), and a couplet about the pleasures of the thighs and mouths of boys in the flower of youth (frg. 25). But much of the poetry is political, either laying down a programme or defending past actions, and it survives because Aristotle's researcher, writing the *Constitution of the Athenians*, and Plutarch, writing his *Life of Solon*, read and quoted it. In these poems we have a master of 'spin' at work; we are hardly getting an objective description of Solon's political actions but we are being given a very good indication of the political issues.

Solon appears to have been archon in Athens in 594. Whether at that time or at another, and debate on this has been lively but inconsequential, he was given responsibility for revising Athenian laws and for making some sweeping constitutional innovations. He assumed those powers because of a political crisis to which there seem to have been social and economic aspects. Solon himself writes (frg. 36W, quoted by [Aristotle] *Constitution of the Athenians* 12.4) of tearing up boundary stones fixed in the black earth, and of bringing back to Attica men who had been sold into slavery, and later tradition (e.g. [Aristotle] *Constitution of the Athenians* 2.2) talks of mysterious 'sixth-parters' (*hektemoroi*) whose distress was part of the crisis (and who never reappear in later Athenian history).

Solon's poetry repeatedly stresses his position in the middle of two opposed factions: he is perhaps the first man in western history to boast of finding the third way. In the various passages quoted in chapter 12 of the Aristotelian *Constitution of the Athenians* he compares himself to a wolf surrounded by many dogs, and a boundary stone between armies. He prides himself on having contained the people, claiming that had he given in to either side the city would have lost many men. He complains that everyone regards him with annoyance and insists that he did not give equal shares of the land to the 'bad' as well as the 'good'. As the language of the last claim indicates, Solon is not a man who pretends that class distinctions do not occur. Reading between the lines of the poems, it appears that his strength lay in insisting very firmly on restoring minimum conditions of livelihood to the poor, without thereby under-mining the distinction between the poor and the rich. Whether he abolished debt or redistributed land was already an issue in antiquity, and his poetic language can be argued to support either claim.

The poetry itself does not describe the political institutions of Athens or any of Solon's laws. Solon became to such an extent 'the' lawgiver in Athens that Athenians quite blatantly referred to laws made very much later as 'laws of Solon'. But there are some laws of Solon about which we can be reasonably confident. One concerns 'classes' in Athens. Solon divided the Athenian citizenry into four groups depending on their wealth: the prop-ertyless *thetes* at the bottom, the *zeugites* who became associated with the heavily armed hoplites, the *hippeis* or cavalry, and the *pentakosiomedimnoi* ('500-bushel men') ([Aristotle] *Constitution of the Athenians* 7.3–4). Which class you were in affected what offices you could hold in the state, as well as what branch of the army you were expected to fight in. The Solonian classes have often been taken to be the crucial point at which wealth replaced birth as the criterion for access to political power, but there is no good evidence for a closed aristocracy in Athens before this time. A fragment of the list of Athenian archons (ML6/Fornara 23), inscribed in the late fifth century, includes, probably just before the archonship of Solon, one 'Kuphselos', a man whose name is more likely to represent intermarriage between an Athenian family and the family of Kypselos tyrant of Corinth than mere emulation. The sense of an international élite positively looking to marry each other is reinforced by the story told by Herodotus of Kleisthenes tyrant of Sikyon advertising at the Olympics that he was looking for a husband for his daughter Agariste, and then holding a year-long competition to choose between rival suitors. This is a world in which it was by lifestyle, by being, as the élite claimed to be, 'better', that individuals established their claim to be members of the élite: there were no barriers of genealogy for Solon to break down, and we have already seen that he did not assault the barriers of prejudice.

What Solon's census classes do is what his laws do more generally: they establish measurable criteria. As we have seen, few of his laws abolish the need for judgement to be passed, but they indicate clearly what the judgement is to be about. It came to be the case that both *zeugite* and *hippeis* standards were expressed in measurable form (our sources claim first in *medimnoi* and then in drachmas), but there is reason to believe that they may originally have stood simply as names: you were a *hippeus* by providing a horse and being prepared to serve in the cavalry. Solon's census classes, like his other laws, can be seen to put a limit on the arbitrary, and so to reveal how to ensure that one fell one side rather than another of legal categories. As far as we can see, nothing that Solon did addressed whatever economic roots there may have been to the crisis which he was brought in to deal with. Some of his actions turned back the clock, restoring slaves to their homes and to freedom, restoring land to its freedom (whatever that might mean in detail). Some of his actions prevented a precise repetition of the consequences of economic crisis (no more borrowing money on security of one's own body). But none of these actions attacked any causes of poverty. What Solon did rather was establish a baseline of expectations, and a set of procedures which all citizens could reasonably expect to see followed. Although there is a limit to how systematic Solon was, it appears that in his case, at least, it is reasonable to talk of a law code, and that his laws set out the powers of magistrates one by one in order.

When Aristotle observed that an individual ruler might be safer than written law he was effectively replaying the choice made in archaic Greek communities. Did one go for appointing a lawgiver and sorting out written rules, or did one go for entrusting it all to an individual ruler charismatic enough to convince one that he was 'safe'? That was not a one-off choice, but a choice that remained continually open. The years immediately after Solon's archonship saw two occasions when the Athenians did not manage to make an election to the archonship, and another occasion when the archon clung on to power after the end of the year and was only expelled by force when he had been in office for two years and two months. A generation after Solon's laws, the Athenians came to have a tyrant, Peisistratos, but when Peisistratos' sons, Hipparchos and Hippias, were removed from power by assassination and the Spartans respectively, the constitutional framework which Solon had created proved easily adaptable to give full powers to the people.

Chapter 5

Making enemies

Classical Greeks were conscious that they fought wars in a peculiar way. Herodotus records that when the Persian king Xerxes was contemplating invading Greece he was in part persuaded to do so by a speech given by his general Mardonios. Mardonios draws attention to the Greek propensity for fighting each other and insistence on doing so in strange circumstances: 'they go off and find the finest and most level piece of land they can and have their battle on it' (7.9β1). Almost 300 years later Polybios (18.31), in his account of the Roman conquest of Greece which he himself had witnessed, similarly drew attention to the extreme inflexibility of Greek fighting methods: 'the phalanx [of heavily armed infantry] has only one moment and one kind of place in which it can operate to its own advantage'.

The choice of a manner of fighting which required flat plains, in a land where flat plains were singularly hard to come by, was not the only way in which Greeks came to regard the way in which they fought as perverse. There was also the matter of the rules of engagement. Polybios (13.3), again, stresses that Greek wars knew nothing underhand: battles only happened when the enemy had been given notice by a declaration of war, they did not involve weapons that struck from afar but only hand-to-hand fighting, and the choice of battlefield was agreed in advance. Plutarch, writing 250 years later, again stresses what a friendly business the war between Corinth and Megara had been, three-quarters of a millennium before his time (*Greek Questions* 17).

None of these descriptions of how the Greeks fought wars is simply a description. In all cases the ancient Greek manner of fighting is being described in opposition to another manner of fighting. Mardonios is describing Greek warfare in implicit contrast with Persian warfare: Greeks fight in so preposterous a way that they will be easy to beat. Polybios is explaining why the Greek hoplite phalanx was unable to resist the Roman invaders. Plutarch is explaining particular phrases by drawing attention to aspects of early Greek warfare that would seem entirely alien to his readers in Roman Greece.

In the case of Herodotus and Polybios, at least, the description of warfare is itself part of the warfare. That is, understanding how the Persians saw Greek warfare is part of understanding the course of the subsequent Persian invasion of Greece. Understanding how, in changed circumstances, the manner of warfare which had proved adequate to defend Greece on earlier occasions proved inadequate to defend her against Rome is integral to understanding the narrative of Roman conquest which Polybios is giving. To explain how you fight a war, or to explain how others fight wars, is never a neutral matter, it is always part of setting up the opposition between conflicting sides. It serves variously to justify the conflict, its causes and its course.

It is in the light of this that we need to return to Plutarch's account of early Greek warfare. The wars of archaic Greek history tend to be precisely wars like the one he describes, in so far as they are wars between neighbours. But they tend to be like that because such stories were useful. Tradition told that the Euboian cities of Chalkis and Eretria clashed in a war over the Lelantine plain. One of the few pieces of 'data' that we have about this war, which historians tend to think was a series of clashes in the first half of the seventh century, is a claim in Strabo's *Geography*, written at the end of the first century BC, that a Euboean inscription recorded that the two sides agreed not to use weapons that strike from afar. This inscription is far more likely to be a later reconstruction of earlier history than it is to be something inscribed in the seventh century. In fact, it plausibly derives from some lines of the seventh-century poet Archilochos in which he celebrates the fact that the spear-famed lords of Euboia fight with swords and not with slings or bows (3W). Turning such an earlier description into a prescription will not have happened by chance; most plausibly it occurred in a context in which neighbourly relations were again at issue.

One particularly complicated war between neighbours is that between Sparta and Tegea as told by Herodotus (1.66–8). To explain how Sparta came to be the pre-eminent power in the Peloponnese at the time, in the middle of the sixth century, when the Lydian king Kroisos was looking for Greek allies for his war against Persia, Herodotus tells how Peloponnesian cities became subject to Sparta, using Tegea as his example. The Spartans, he tells, initially wanted to enslave their Tegean neighbours, but they were unsuccessful and only succeeded in having their own soldiers put to slavish work by the Tegeans. Only, to put a modern gloss on Herodotus' account of the discovery of the 'bones of Orestes', when the Spartans accompanied war by diplomatic moves which stressed common ancestry were they successful, that is, only when the war was no longer a matter of annexation but of securing an alliance, albeit a one-sided one. In this case too a later source, this time Plutarch, claims that there was an inscription that related to this war, an inscription which suggests (probably, the interpretation is disputed) that Sparta's action with Tegea was motivated by a concern that the subject population of Messenia not be offered a route to freedom through the Arkadian city. Once more, we may be concerned here with an inscription put up later to offer a past template for current action (or inaction), but what is important is that, according to fifth-century and later Greeks, archaic wars happened between neighbours and usually did not lead to the conquest of the defeated enemy.

We see this pattern again in the claims made about another conflict between Sparta and a neighbour, this time Argos. According to this story, once more told in the first book of Herodotus (1.82), Sparta had already taken over a piece of land that had once been in Argive control, the territory of Thyrea. The Argives, wanting it back, marched out against the Spartans, and came to an agreement that the fate of the territory could be decided in a battle between 300 chosen warriors from each side. In the battle all were killed except for one man on each side. The Spartan survivor remained on the battlefield and claimed the victory, the Argive ran home to say that he was victorious. Since they could not decide between the claims otherwise, the Argives and Spartans then fought a full-scale battle, in which the Spartans were victorious. Thyrea remained in Spartan hands.

It would not be hard to multiply these stories, but the pattern should already be clear. Classical Greeks wanted to believe of their past that neighbours had often settled scores by warfare, but that the warfare had been conducted according to strong conventions about fairness, and had been more concerned with the relative statuses of the parties than with taking over other cities, although marginal adjustments of border territory might result.

The exceptions to this tradition show up the political significance of the standard version. There came to be, for example, a tradition that Sparta had conquered and taken over neighbouring Messenia. War between the two is alluded to in the poetry of Tyrtaios, written in the seventh century, but the only full account that survives for us is in Pausanias, writing in the second century AD. Pausanias' sources go back at best to the hellenistic period, and arguably he has extensively rehandled them. It is at least highly likely that Messenia only acquired a history of its subjugation at the time when it was liberated, in the fourth century BC, when the Thebans saw to the creation of an independent Messenia in order permanently to weaken Sparta. Stories of conquest keep alive traditions of resistance: there were good reasons for traditions of conflict to survive only in cases where both parties involved could claim to have come out of the conflict with some grounds for pride. Where one side was effectively subjugated, as in this case, the war survived in memory only for a generation or so, and had to be reinvented when changed political circumstances gave the Messenians the opportunity to reinvent a past by which they could justify their new status.

The conflict between Sparta and Messenia is an exception to the general pattern because it involves subjugation of one party by another. The story of conflict between Phokis and Thessaly is an exception because, although the result is the usual stalemate, the means by which stalemate is reached is trickery. The context in which Herodotus (8.27–30) tells us about the way in which Phokis had resisted military pressure from her much larger northern neighbour, Thessaly, is precisely the context of the Persian Wars, in which the people of Thessaly supported the Persians, and the Phokians were part of the Greek resistance. Herodotus tells the story as part of his claim that it was hatred of Thessaly, rather than any other reason, which caused the Phokians to fight against Persia. This claim has a particularly literary value in Herodotus' account, since it follows a story in which a Persian, on hearing that the Greeks compete at the Olympic games for a wreath and not for money, exclaims 'Good heavens, Mardonios, what sort of men have you brought us to fight against, who hold contests not for money but about excellence!' (8.26). Herodotus is undercutting this view of the morality of Greek competitiveness by noting that that competitiveness could lead to behaviour in which moral considerations played no part. More generally, telling stories of Phokian trickery enabled the Thessalians to explain the inexplicable – how a place like Phokis could resist the might of Thessalian cavalry – and it enabled the Phokians to maintain a reputation for barring no holds which itself could serve to keep potential enemies at bay.

Whether we consider what I have described as the standard pattern, or whether we consider aberrant examples such as that concerning Phokis and Thessaly, it makes sense to look at the wars of the archaic period as a symbolic expression because it was as symbols that classical Greeks needed those wars. For this reason we should not be so very surprised that few fifth- and fourth-century conflicts between Greek cities quite fit the pattern alleged for the earlier period. When Sparta clashes again with Argos, perhaps in the 490s, the keynote of the narrative is not fairness but deceit: Kleomenes the king of Sparta gets his men to attack at a moment when he knows the Argive troops to be breakfasting, and when the surprised Argive army tries to run away they are trapped and massacred, first by straight deceit and then by getting helots (whose servile status meant that they could be treated as non-persons and set up to attract the wrath of the gods with impunity) to set fire to a sacred grove (Herodotus 6.78, 7.148). Xenophon's account of an occasion in the fourth century when the Spartan king Agesipolis invaded Argos makes it clear that the extent to which even religious factors were allowed to interfere with the waging of war depended entirely on what the army commander decided – sacred truces could be rejected, earthquakes taken as bad or good omens, bad sacrifices made an excuse for ending a campaign (*Hellenica* 4.7.3–7). We can no more take these accounts to be objective than we can take the accounts of archaic wars to be objective, but they do show how classical Greeks were perfectly aware of the degree to which contemporary warfare might be anything but a straight-up-and-down fight.

But if the claims about wars always having been fought in a gentlemanly way were largely wishful thinking on the part of the Greeks, the more general observation that Greek cities fought each other with heavily armed infantry in a landscape which might be thought very much better suited to action by light-armed troops remained largely true. Why did Greek cities not fight in a way more adapted to the rugged land they lived in?

The choice of mode of warfare has to be understood in terms of the manpower available to fight, and the reasons for fighting. The men who defended the city as soldiers were the same men who kept the city alive by their labours in the fields. This was partly a matter of an agricultural régime which was labour-intensive, partly a concern for the possible effects of arming those who had no stake in the land for which they fought. The consequence was that cities were in a position to put an army into the field only when the citizens did not need to be in the field for agricultural purposes. The only exception to this was Sparta. The existence of a subjugated population of helots, and the possession of a vast territory from which a large non-labouring body of Spartan citizens could be supported, meant that all adult Spartans could spend their time training for war. This should have meant that the Spartans were free to fight at every season, but in fact they needed support from allies who were not in the same happy position, and also feared that prolonged absence of large numbers of Spartan citizens might encourage helot revolt, so that Spartans were no more flexible over the timing of their warfare than other cities. Since the campaigning season was short, military confrontations needed to be brisk and decisive. The sort of prolonged campaign familiar in light-armed guerrilla warfare in mountainous territory was in no one's interests. Similarly, guerrilla warfare suits wars of attrition, in which what is being sought is the capitulation of the enemy, but in many wars between Greek cities what was at issue was not securing total surrender but securing a change in the border, a change of political régime, or a demonstration of superiority in the face of rival claims from a neighbour. Guerrilla warfare also suits situations where forces are ill-matched: small numbers of light-armed guerrilla troops can cause havoc to a very much larger opposing force. But, with the exception of Athens, and to some extent Sparta, Greek cities were all relatively small, and when a larger city faced a smaller one there were usually other neighbours keen to join in resisting the larger city before it turned on them. In the light of all this, it made excellent sense for the farmers, who were also the citizen body, to march in and ravage the fields that were the basis for the neighbouring city's livelihood, and to be met by the farmers, who were also the citizen body, fighting for the fields that they farmed.

There is a lot of evidence that minor warfare between neighbours continued to be a frequent feature of fifth- and fourth-century Greek history. In the 490s the Persian administrator

Artaphernes got so fed up with the constant raiding of each other's territory by the Greeks of Ionia that he compelled them to submit to arbitration and insisted on measuring out borders which each city was to respect (Herodotus 6.42). In the 390s the cities of southern Greece were drawn into a general war that began as simply the latest in a series of border raids between Phokis and Lokris (Xenophon *Hellenica* 3.5.3–4, *Hellenica Oxyrhynchia* 18). In a slight variation on the pattern, it was with the assistance of mercenaries that the people of Kleitor in Arkadia fought the people of neighbouring Orchomenos in the 370s, despite the fact that both were allies of Sparta. (We hear about this only because Sparta decided she needed the mercenaries for her own campaign against Thebes, Xenophon *Hellenica* 5.4.36.)

The wars that dominate fifth- and fourth-century history, however, were quite different from any of the traditions. They were different in scale, different in manner, and different in aim. What changed things was the threat of Persia. During the seventh century and the first half of the sixth century the major power immediately adjacent to the Greek cities of Anatolia was Lydia. The Greeks knew Lydia as a place of great wealth ruled by massively rich and powerful men. Relations between Greek cities and Lydia were not always good. Gyges had captured the city of Kolophon, his successor Ardys captured Priene, and two generations further on Alyattes captured Smyrna. All three of these Lydian kings attacked Miletos (unsuccessfully). But these wars were not terribly different from wars between neighbouring Greek cities, and the Lydians were far from enjoying uniformly hostile relations with the Greeks: several Lydian rulers made dedications at Greek sanctuaries or consulted Greek oracles (even if they did not really understand how oracles worked), and at least some of those who visited the Lydian king came away very much enriched. Something of the cultural interchange between Greeks and Lydians emerges from the history of coinage. It is quite likely that the world's first coins were minted around 600 BC, by the Lydians, as indeed ancient sources claim; but it was in the temple of Artemis at Ephesos that the earliest known coins were found, and it is in the Greek world that the numismatic habit spread at a very rapid rate.

In the middle of the sixth century Kroisos, as king of Lydia, decided to attack the great power to his east, Persia. Much of the first book of Herodotus is taken up with the story of Kroisos, of his attempt to discover the future by consulting oracles (unaware that what oracles do is help you decide the better of two options, not tell you what is best absolutely), of his being told by the Delphic oracle that if he attacked the Persians he would destroy a great empire, and of his attacking and destroying a great empire – his own. History and fiction are intertwined in this story (we have already met the impossible story of a conversation between Solon and Kroisos), but that Persia defeated Lydia is certain. That defeat changed Greek history.

It was not so much that the Persians were actively interventionist, more that they were prepared to intervene. As a result they found themselves brought in by factions and individuals keen to secure their position in their own cities by being able to call upon Persian support if they faced too much local opposition. Herodotus (4.136–7) tells the story of various tyrants of Ionian cities being recruited to support a Persian campaign against Scythia in the last but one decade of the sixth century. These tyrants were left to guard the bridge over the Danube while King Darius led his Persian troops further north. When Darius does not return promptly the Scythians suggest to them that they should abandon their position and hence abandon Darius to his fate. But the tyrant of Miletos, Histiaios, points out to the others that if Darius perishes so do they: their position depends upon their being seen as well-connected at the Persian court and able to command suitable military support.

But the situation of the puppet ruler is not a comfortable one, and within two decades of Darius' rather disastrous Scythian campaign the Greek cities of Ionia mounted a revolt led, it seems, by one of those tyrants. What exactly the revolt was about is not easy to discover. We have only one substantial account of the revolt, in the pages of Herodotus (5.28–6.32). Herodotus states in his preface that his work concerns the great and marvellous deeds of Greeks and barbarians, and in particular the reasons why they went to war with each other. The Ionian revolt, as it is called, is for him an essential preliminary to the Persian wars proper, that is to the Persian invasion of Greece. He calls the revolt, indeed, the 'beginning of evils'. But the Ionian revolt is also for him an example of how not to fight a war, and his account points up the disunity of the Ionians as a contrast to the, actually very limited, unity of the Greeks. It is the ability of some Greek states to put their enmities behind them and concert their efforts against the Persians that Herodotus sees, and surely correctly, as essential to Greek success against the Persian invader. Many have therefore thought his account of the Ionian revolt to be biased, for it emphasises personal motives for starting the revolt and the unwillingness of the Ionians to endure the sorts of discipline necessary to carry it through. Indeed there are some grounds for wondering whether the rather disparate anti-Persian actions spread over several years that are put together as 'the Ionian revolt' should be seen as a single revolt at all – the very creation of 'a revolt' may have been a product of the desire to point up the parallels with 'the Persian War' in Greece.

Scepticism, and searching for explanations not contemplated by Herodotus, such as that the Persians were squeezing Ionian trade, can be overdone. There is no doubt that two mainland cities, Athens and Eretria, did provide military help to the Ionians against the Persians, and this itself implies some concerted action. There is equally no doubt that the revolt included an attack upon the provincial capital, Sardis, which was burned. Such an attack was pointlessly provocative unless part of a wholehearted effort to persuade the Persians to abandon the whole region. Nor was such an effort necessarily folly. Darius did not have an easy reign: an inscription from Bisitun (Brosius (2000) no. 44), in recording the number of 'pretenders' to power whom he had crushed, also shows how very common revolt was within the Persian empire. The story of a tyrant who had been removed to the Persian capital as a 'reward', and who then sent a secret message to encourage revolt, in order in that way to secure his own return to the region, may be the stuff of fiction, but it well reveals the tensions on both sides in a régime of puppet governments.

In 494 a major battle and the capture and destruction of the great city of Miletos effectively ended the Ionian revolt. The Persians tried new tactics in ruling Ionia, reassessing taxes and supporting popular power rather than tyrants. They strengthened the power that they had already acquired in Thrace, on the European side of the Hellespont. They also organised an attack on mainland Greece, mounting a seaborne invasion. That invasion succeeded in laying waste the city of Eretria on Euboia, but when it landed in Attica it was defeated, against the odds, in the plain of Marathon.

In the much-quoted view of J.S. Mill, in a review of George Grote's great nineteenth-century *History of Greece*, the battle of Marathon was a more important event in English history than the battle of Hastings. The argument in support of this is that, had the Persians won, Greece would have become part of an oriental empire and none of the intellectual and cultural developments of the fifth century would have occurred. But there is something to be said for a diametrically opposed view – that losing the battle of Marathon would have caused much less trouble than winning it. Had the Athenians been beaten and Athens set ablaze, that might have been the end of the business. Honour would have been satisfied on the Persian side and, what with Darius dying shortly afterwards, the west might have faded from Persian view. There would have been no need for the great Persian invasion of 480, and without the invasion there would have been no concerted Greek resistance, no building up of a naval force by Athens or inspiring naval victory, no ongoing naval campaign to remove Persian influence from the Greek cities of Ionia and elsewhere.

How plausible this alternative view of the importance of the battle of Marathon is depends in part on second-guessing the Persians. Since virtually all our evidence for the Persians comes from Greek sources, this is very difficult to do. Although Darius starts by looking for token submission from Greeks (the giving of earth and water), it is highly plausible that, as in Ionia so in the Greek mainland, disaffected individuals leaving their home cities and going to the Persian king to seek support (as Hippias did when ousted from Athens, or the Spartan king Demaratos when removed from his throne in Sparta) would, sooner or later, have occasioned direct Persian intervention. But the main value of this counterfactual history is to draw attention to the transformative effect of the Greek campaign against the Persian invaders in 480–479 and its success.

The Persian invasion of 480 was a combined invasion by land and sea, not directly across the Aegean, as in 490, but through Thrace and Macedonia and then south. Greek cities had long been expecting this invasion, and they had a chance both to build up their own military resources (Athens massively expanded her navy and this is unlikely to have been prompted by a quarrel with neighbouring Aigina alone) and to muster some semblance of united resistance. An attempt to resist the Persians at Thermopylae, in a narrow defile, was foiled by the Persians discovering a way round, and left the Greeks with a heroic myth of Spartans fighting to the death, but nothing more. The whole of Greece north and east of the isthmus of Corinth was abandoned to the Persians, who sacked the city of Athens. But further advance was stemmed, first by a massive naval victory in the waters between the mainland and the island of Salamis, where the Persian fleet had managed to get itself trapped, and then, in the following season, by a straightforward hoplite defeat of the remaining Persian forces in the plains of Boiotia at Plataia. The Persians then retreated leaving behind enough precious metals, etc., significantly to enrich the Greeks, but also a more important legacy in the armies that had defeated them.

The Greeks had no way of knowing in 479 that the Persians would not return to make a further attempt at conquest. Those who argued that attack was the best form of defence, and that the campaign should be continued at least until Persian overlordship was removed from the Greek cities of the Aegean and

Anatolia, won the day. But any such ongoing campaign had to be a naval campaign, and that meant that it was bound to be led by the major naval power, Athens, not the major infantry power, Sparta. Athens took over the campaign, and delivered freedom from Persia in a long series of campaigns. These culminated after about fifteen years in a great battle off the mouth of the river Eurymedon in southern Anatolia, but continued after that, by way of unsuccessful attempts to foment rebellion in Egypt, conquered by Persia in the sixth century but ever volatile, to a probable formal peace in 451. Such continuous campaigning demanded that a high degree of unity be maintained, at least among those who stood to gain or lose from the result, and Athens policed that unity extremely vigorously, coercing cities to join the 'Delian League', to give it its modern name, making them contribute either ships or, more frequently, money payments, and preventing them from leaving. Freedom from Persia went together with a relationship of obligation to Athens.

The effective transformation of Athens from a large, but militarily rather unimportant, city, as in the sixth century, to a massively powerful force had a marked effect both on Athens itself and on relations between Greek cities in the mainland. In the case of Athens itself a major part of the impact was the conse- quence of the size and military importance of her navy. To serve as a hoplite required personal wealth in order to afford the equip- ment; but anyone could serve as a rower, and Athens needed so many rowers (a fleet of 100 ships required upwards of 15,000 rowers) that poor, and not so poor, citizens, foreigners, and slaves were all paid to pull the oar. For many, a summer season in the triremes came to be an integral part of their livelihood. And if this gave the Athenian assembly reason to vote for further warfare it also created enormous demands for financial and other plan- ning: merely to keep a large fleet afloat demanded administrative organisation on an unheard-of scale. For the first time ever, a Greek state acquired something that could be called a bureau- cracy – for all that it remained mainly in the hands of citizens who were generally chosen by lot and served only for a year. The way in which the Athenians imagined themselves hardly kept up with the change: the images on monuments to the war dead continue to show hoplites and cavalry, and only in contexts of comparison with other Greeks is the considerable skill required to man a trireme stressed at all. Even Thucydides' analysis fails to bring out the extent to which it was skilled financial administration (and the lucky accident of Athens' silver resources) that was now crucial.

As to the relations between Greek cities, transferring the war against Persia to the sea turned Sparta and Athens from allies into permanent adversaries. They clashed for the first time in an infantry battle at Tanagra in Boiotia in 457/6, nearly came to battle again a decade later, and for the whole of the last third of the fifth century were almost continuously at war. Thucydides, who was briefly an Athenian general in that war and wrote an account of it, suggests that it was fear of growing Athenian power that brought the war about. This is a rather unsatisfactory explanation as to why war was declared in 432 BC in particular, but it accurately picks out what had changed in Greek history.

In the sixth century Sparta had built up a series of allies, largely, it seems, in order to ensure that the subject population of Messenia had no one to turn to for support or refuge. Although those allies had been mobilised from time to time to take action against other cities – against Argos, for instance, or against Athens at the end of the sixth century – the Peloponnesian League, as scholars have called it, did not radically change the conditions of warfare. But Athens' formation of the 'Delian League' was a different matter. Whereas Sparta merely requested allied support for its actions and had to listen to its allies' views on whether action should be taken or not, Athens' allies effectively had no say in the actions of the Delian League; they were compelled to pay their (relatively modest) dues and had to dance to whatever tune Athens played. Athens took a strongly interventionist policy and its demands for regular tribute from its allies gave it an unparalleled resource base. No single city could reckon to stand up to the Athenians, and in consequence those not prepared to join Athens looked for support elsewhere, and if they could they allied themselves to Sparta. The Greek world became polarised between those who were with Athens and those who were with Sparta, and the sort of conflict between neighbours that had previously been inconsequential now became potentially a cause of a major Greek war. But the lines of this conflict were not merely formed over foreign policy. Athens promoted, although not systematically or even consistently, popular rule, whereas Sparta became associated with the rule of the few, keen that among its allies power should be in the hands of a small group whom Sparta could control through the sanctions of friendship. The Greek world became ideologically split, and within a single city different groups would favour Athenians or Spartans according to their preference for popular or élite rule. The personal politics, which dominated the archaic Greek world, were subordinated to a politics in which the argument was framed, at least, in terms of principles.

Chapter 6

The city of freedom and oppression

Freedom is the watchword of Greek politics in the fifth century. We have already met Demaratos, the ex-king of Sparta, telling Xerxes that by Sparta's valour Greece now keeps both poverty and bondage at bay and that the Dorian Greeks, at least, will not under any circumstances accept terms which would mean slavery for Greece. In his own voice Herodotus praises Athens on the grounds that it was her decision to preserve Greek freedom that determined that the Persians would be resisted and beaten. In 432 the Spartans went to war with Athens again to preserve Greek freedom, but at the end of the first year of the war, at the annual burial of the war dead, it is the Athenian political leader Pericles who is recorded by Thucydides as having given the speech that has come to be the centrepiece of defences of western liberty. The exposition, and usually the extolling, of Greek freedom has proved irresistible to generations of ancient historians.

Freedom goes hand in hand with oppression. Only the threat of oppression makes freedom worth mentioning. More than that, only oppression sustains it; oppression is built into the very structures which are held to guarantee freedom.

The structures of the classical Athenian constitution were laid down primarily in the reforms of Kleisthenes at the end of the sixth century. Liberated from the tyranny of Hippias in 510, Athens had fallen back into a pattern of factional disputes not dissimilar to that which was said to have formed the background to the seizure of power by Peisistratos in the first place. But Kleisthenes' solution to this was to render real the explicit extension of power to the people that had become statutory with Solon. This involved most particularly setting up a Council which drew its members proportionately from each of the demes, that is the villages of Attica and separate neighbourhoods within the town of Athens itself. This Council set the agenda for, and saw to the execution of, the decisions of the Assembly of citizens, into whose hands the final decisions on virtually all major matters came to be entrusted. Becoming an Athenian citizen and eligible to attend the Assembly was primarily a matter of being recognised in one's deme as of Athenian parentage (initially on the father's side, and then from the middle of the fifth century on both father's and mother's sides) and eighteen years of age. Serving in the Council depended on being over the age of thirty, and then being selected by lot from the members of one's deme who had not already served twice in that capacity.

This structure enforced widespread active participation on the part of a large percentage of the Athenian citizen body. About 20,000 Athenian citizens were required to ensure that the Athenian Council could be filled from citizens serving only once in a lifetime. Universal service on the Council, which demanded being in the town of Athens virtually every day of the year, can never have been achieved, but except when Athens was at its most populous, in the period from c.460 to the plague of 430, it is implausible that fewer than a third to a half of citizens took their turn in the Council. This is a very high level of popular political participation indeed.

High levels of participation in the Council, and a people's assembly that insisted on taking all major decisions, went together with popular law courts. Some sort of popular court seems to have existed from the time of Solon, but it may have been only from the shadowy political reforms of the late 460s associated with Ephialtes that the court of the Areopagus, which was an élite body made up of those who had previously been one of the nine archons, the chief magistrates of Athens, became restricted to hearing cases involving homicide (a role which it fulfils, hardly coincidentally, in Aeschylus' *Eumenides*). From that time on it was courts manned by large groups (201, 501 and even larger) who saw to the administration of justice in Athens. The jurors for any particular case were selected by lot from a panel of Athenians over the age of thirty who had taken the juror's oath, who were distributed at random to particular cases. The jurors heard the cases and reached their decision without discussion and without judges or professional lawyers.

An increasingly large body of citizen administrators was involved in the day-to-day running of the city. This was entrusted not to single magistrates but boards of magistrates. The use of boards seems to have been a practice going back into the archaic period, a product perhaps of the competitive distrust of influential Athenians for one another, parallels to which we have seen in the legislation also of other cities. How many administrative offices there were in Athens in 500 is very uncertain, but the Aristotelian *Constitution of the Athenians* claims that at the height of the Athenian empire 700 Athenians were employed in offices in Athens and 700 abroad, and these are not implausible figures.

It is easy to see how these structures were liberating. There were still some qualifications for office, both qualifications of age, as mentioned above, and qualifications of wealth (only the rich were eligible to handle large quantities of money, either in the charming but surely naïve belief that they were less corruptible or simply because only those who had money of their own had the right experience with monetary sums). These formal barriers were ignored in practice, and what barriers there were to a citizen participating in the running of the city at every level were practical, not legal. Some of the practical barriers were at least lowered by local practice: by the fourth century, at least, the individual demes had developed structures (deme assemblies, deme magistracies) that were closely parallel to the structures of the city, so that the local community offered at least some sort of political education to prepare a citizen for full participation in what must have been the much more daunting setting of the Assembly on the Pnyx or Council in the Agora.

Athenian democracy offered opportunities and made demands different from those made by modern western democracy. Modern democracies are openly factional; they rely upon political parties, which organise opinion, and elections, in which people choose between different programmes that have, traditionally, explicitly served the interests of some parts of the citizen body more than others. In Athens there were no formal parties, and any hint of a group 'organising the vote' was taken as a threat to the system. It had to be. Unlike the citizens of current western states, citizens were expected to have political initiative, and to surrender that initiative, as one does when joining a 'party', was seen as a threat to the system. As we saw in chapter 1, the man who prostituted himself was prohibited from speaking in public – precisely because he had shown himself ready to surrender his initiative, to be bought.

Modern democracies take voting to be a right, part of the right to self-determination. But voting in Athenian democracy was not simply a matter of voting in elections. To be a citizen was, in the phrases used by Aristotle, 'to share in government' and 'to rule and be ruled in turn'. To justify such a role for citizens requires more than merely belief in a right to self-determination, it demands a belief that all citizens have basic political capabilities. This is not something that was simply taken for granted, but is argued for very explicitly in a speech put into the mouth of the philosopher Protagoras in the dialogue which Plato names after him. Protagoras, who was from Abdera and not himself an Athenian, claims that everyone has a sense of justice, or fairness, and of shame, and it is those moral and intellectual qualities that are sufficient, as well as necessary, for the performance of the citizen's duties.

But Athenian democracy demanded more equality than simply the possession of a 'minimum kit' in the form of a common sense of justice and shame. Fully participatory democracy breaks down once factionalism breaks out. Every democratic decision will leave dissatisfied the minority who voted against the decision. If that minority is always made up of the same people, then problems arise. A tyrannous majority, which pursues factional interests at the expense of a minority, renders hollow any claim to democracy. Athenians had to believe that they had a single set of interests, and that differences of opinion were differences about how best to serve those interests, not differences about what the interests were. For the Marxist this is to say that Athenian democracy depended on 'false consciousness': 'class' interests needed to be suppressed and all to believe that they shared interests with all Athenian citizens and not just with some. Such trust had to be sustained, and all who entered the Assembly in order to join in a debate had to believe that every individual present would listen to the arguments and decide accordingly, and not on the basis of preconceived positions. Dissent was the essence of debate and the Athenians prided themselves on the possibility of frank speech, but it was essential that that dissent was non-systematic and did not question citizen equality. Ignoring differences was achieved in part by conventions about what were the proper areas for political intervention: foreign policy absorbed a very great deal of political debate, local social and economic issues were very largely avoided.

Sustaining the belief that politics was for everyone required a much stronger sense of citizen equality than is required in modern rights-based notions of equality. Athenians had to believe in an equality that was substantive: that all citizens could take equal part in politics at every level. The system did indeed come to include some measures to ensure that equality could be made operational: probably from the 450s onwards holding magisterial office in Athens, including serving on the Council, was paid, as was serving as a juror in the courts. And in the fourth century pay was introduced for attending the Assembly. The introduction of such practical measures to enable participation itself acknowledged that not all citizens were equal. Some could afford to take an active part in political life, others could do so only if given financial assistance. Even then, serving as a juror came to be, Aristophanes' *Wasps* suggests, notoriously a retirement pursuit, a source of pension for those no longer able to labour with their bodies. But the inequalities acknowledged and observed in these ways remained practical inequalities which could be practically overcome. What Athenian democracy had to resist was the suggestion that there might be relevant inequalities, inequalities of intelligence for instance, that could not be overcome.

The demands that participatory democracy made on the Athenians resulted in both repression and oppression. Repression because there were certain things that could not be acknowledged. When resistance to democracy occurred, as it did in 411 and 404 when democracy was briefly replaced by oligarchy, that resistance had to be seen as a consequence of a conspiracy of particular individuals, not a product of a 'class' rising, and the punitive reaction was therefore visited upon individuals. Repression too because the different interests of different social groups could never be fully acknowledged in political discussion: so, for example, to be an Athenian was always envisioned as to be a heavily armed soldier, even though many Athenians served not in the infantry but in the fleet.

More serious was the oppression. M.I. Finley famously remarked that the growth of freedom and the growth of slavery went hand in hand. In saying this he was thinking of the demand for slave labour created by the need for citizen leisure sufficient to enable participation in the Assembly, Council, and various offices of democracy. But there is a more general sense in which this is true. For it to be possible to imagine that all citizens were substantively equal there had to be no situation in which one citizen was manifestly under the thumb of another. Claims of equality could not be maintained in the face of one citizen exercising corporal punishment over another, or of one citizen being the servant of another, or one citizen owning a silver mine and another working in the unhealthy and unpleasant mining galleries. For citizens to be equal demanded that there were others to do the 'dirty work', and in Athens those others were slaves.

Slaves are already on the scene in the *Iliad* and *Odyssey*. Men and women captured in war are sold as slaves. Phoenician ships kidnap individuals and sell them on. Solon's abolition of debt bondage implies that by 600 the enslavement of one Greek by another in circumstances other than warfare had become a significant problem. Of the scale of slavery in sixth-century Athens we have little idea, but even to make Kleisthenic democracy thinkable few demeaning tasks can have been in the hands of freeborn Athenians.

Slave numbers are hard to estimate even in classical Athens. That well-off citizens had large numbers of slaves in their households is clear. Those found guilty of damaging the religious statues of Hermes and of parodying the mystery cult at Eleusis in 415 (the so-called 'Mutilation of the Herms and profanation of the Mysteries') had their confiscated property listed in the Eleusinion at Athens, and surviving fragments of those lists include large numbers of slaves, sold at various prices which no doubt reflected experience and skills. All those slaves come from outside the world of the Greek city; they come from the north, from Macedonia, Illyria, Thrace and Scythia, and from the east, Lydia, Caria, Colchis, Phrygia and Syria.

Many slaves were involved in craft production. A shield factory owned by the father of Lysias the orator, who was a resident foreigner, a metic, and not an Athenian citizen, employed 120 slaves, and other establishments of somewhat smaller size are known from fourth-century oratory. Slaves were found in even greater numbers in the silver mines. Xenophon in his *Ways and Means* suggests that there might be employment for 10,000 slaves in the mines, and the extent of the surviving surface and sub-surface workings suggests that his estimate is probably not far from the historical total.

In household tasks, and in the heavier industrial occupations, the labour force was probably almost exclusively slave. But this was not true of all slave occupations. Slaves are found in the accounts for the building of the Erechtheum, the last temple to be built on the Acropolis in the programme of restoring Athens' premier sanctuary to the glory destroyed by the Persians, a programme that had begun with the building of the Parthenon. The Erechtheum accounts show that slaves, metics and citizens all worked on the building works, with a slave and his master often working side by side. Such a situation must also have prevailed in agriculture. There has been much debate about the extent to which Athenian agriculture depended upon slavery, but there seem to me to be strong arguments that, at least at the labour-intensive seasons of sowing and harvest (not just grain harvest but also the vintage and the olive harvest), the whole of the household labour force, including slaves and women, would be mobilised.

If citizen conditions of life had to be seen to be comparable, slave conditions varied enormously. In comedy we mainly see personal slaves, at the beck and call of a capricious and often cowardly master, subject to physical punishment and hard labour, and ever inclined to sleep on the job. But even within the household, affective bonds could be formed. A fourth-century law-court speech reveals the case of a slave nurse who was freed when the children she cared for grew up, left the household and married. In old age, when she was widowed, the child she had looked after took her back into his family and looked after her (Demosthenes 47.55). Such a story may not be typical, but it cannot have been unique.

For male slaves, being well treated by the owner might have even more dramatic consequences. The most remarkable case concerns two slaves involved in banking, Pasion and Phormio. Pasion, born around 430 BC, was the slave of a banker, Archestratos, and on Archestratos' death it was he, now manumitted, rather than Archestratos' son, who was given the banking business to run. Pasion subsequently acquired citizenship in recognition of his financial contributions to Athens' military and naval activities. When he died he passed on both the banking business and his wife Archippe to his own slave, Phormio, rather than to his elder son, Apollodoros, until his younger son, Pasikles, should come of age. Apollodoros much resented this move and created considerable trouble for Phormio in the courts, which is why we know so much about this case. In due course Phormio too gained citizenship as a result of benefactions to Athens, and, like Apollodoros, he seems to have carried out assiduously his duties as a wealthy Athenian. Apollodoros, unlike Phormio, combined financial contributions to Athens with activity in the law courts, and a number of speeches by him are preserved among the speeches attributed to Demosthenes.

Banking was no doubt a special case because of the expertise that it required, and upward mobility from slave to citizen is otherwise almost unheard of in Athens, but that it was possible in these cases indicates the skills and responsibilities that slaves could carry. Significant numbers of slaves were indeed left to work on their own, without constant overlordship. Such slaves, known as slaves who 'lived apart' (*khoris oikountes*), were generally skilled workers who could expect to keep a proportion of what they earned, while their owners remained responsible for their debts. Other slaves were owned by the state, for in so far as there was a civil service in Athens it was a slave civil service. These public slaves tended to be given great responsibility and rather little oversight, not least because the citizen magistrates with whom they worked changed so frequently – ten times a year in some cases, annually in others.

What was life like in this slave society? For 'slave society' it surely was, not only because of the proportion of slaves but also because of their essential structural role. Two passages from classical Athenian literature offer some insight. One of Demosthenes' speeches concerns the case of a man who was beaten up when walking near the Agora. In sketching the background of hostility between him and the man he claims led the gang that mugged him, the speaker tells the story of how he had done military service along with the sons of his assailant at the fort at Panakton on the Athenian border. Those boys, drunk already by supper time, claimed that the speaker's slaves were sending smoke in their direction, beat them up, and kicked over their chamber pots and urinated over the slaves themselves (Demosthenes 54.3–4). The speaker claims that he initially dismissed this behaviour, only complaining to the general when it became persistent. The second passage comes from a curious pamphlet, preserved in the writings of Xenophon, which goes under the title *Constitution of Athens*. This work is an explanation of the logic of Athenian democracy, addressed to those who cannot understand why men like the writer, who do not approve of the system, fail to overthrow it. In the course of the description, the author remarks that slaves and metics in Athens are particularly insubordinate since people do not hit them because they cannot be sure they have rightly distinguished slaves, freedmen and metics from citizens, given that all wear the same poor clothes (*Constitution of Athens* 1.10). Put together these two comments, both of them no doubt improved in the telling, and one has a picture of a society where, when citizens could recognise slaves, some of them were prepared to treat them to routine and unprovoked abuse, and where the only source of restraint was the fear of turning out to have so treated someone whose body was protected by law. Such a picture is very much of a piece with that offered by comedy, and indeed by representations in both art and literature of slaves having deformed bodies: torture, beating, branding, whipping and hard labour left their marks written on the slave body.

Aristotle talks of slaves as 'living tools' and developed an argument that some humans were 'natural slaves', positively advantaged by having decisions taken for them by others, while other humans became slaves by accident but could and should be free. We know that Aristotle did not himself act as if this were true – he freed his slaves in his will, which was either too late (if they were slaves by accident), or inappropriate (if they were better off being slaves). There is no reason to think that Athenians generally thought in terms of 'natural slaves', but their behaviour was equally contradictory. They were prepared to treat slaves' bodies quite differently from the bodies of free men, but equally prepared to grant, to some slaves at least, freedom – and even citizenship. So they treated slaves as a different sort of person, not just different in degree but different in kind, only to turn round and transform them by an act of manumission.

Physical abuse and grants of freedom are arguably not only contradictory but causally related: Athenians abused slaves because they also freed them. That is, the existence of the possibility that an individual slave might become free, a resident non-Athenian and in exceptionally circumstances even an Athenian, made it vital to stress that slaves as a group were nevertheless quite distinct from the body of citizens. The more slaves did some of the things that citizens did, working with citizens on building projects or even, at least towards the end of the long war with Sparta, serving along with Greeks from other cities as rowers in the Athenian navy, the more it was essential to insist that the citizen labourer or rower was quite different. In other cities the poor were excluded from citizenship entirely or citizens were graded so that, for example, those who engaged in trade or pursued certain professions were excluded from the right to take office as a magistrate (compare Aristotle's *Politics* 1278a15–26). In Sparta citizens, Spartiates, were excluded from any occupation, even farming, and maintained by the labour of the subjugated helot population. But in Athens, where birth and age were the only qualifications deciding citizenship, the unity of the citizen body had to be sustained by the construction of contrasts with others. With every blow delivered to, or threatened upon, the body of a slave Athenians beat into themselves their own essential difference from others and with it their own citizen identity.

If Athenian citizens marked themselves out from slaves by treating slaves as animals, they marked themselves out from free non-Athenian residents and from women by treating them as children. People who were not born in Athens but migrated there from other cities and took up residence in Attica for longer than a month had to pay a poll tax, the *metoikion*. This was exacted at a rate of 1 dr. a month for men and half that rate for women.

This was hardly a heavy tax by modern standards: it works out as equivalent to an income tax rate of 3.3 per cent a year if a metic is earning 1 dr. a day (a fairly standard fifth-century wage). But if there were 10,000 male metics in Athens, and in the late fifth century there were probably more, then the city earned 20 talents a year from this tax – and only the two largest tribute payers in the Athenian empire in 440 contributed more than that. In addition to the tax, metics had to be represented by a citizen *prostates* if they went to court, had to be registered as living in a particular deme, and had no right to own landed property in Athens.

The exclusion of resident foreigners from the citizen body is one that we take for granted, since the same is almost universal practice throughout the world today. We find it easy to understand how those not born and bred in a country might be considered not to have sufficient stake in that country to justify their taking part in the decision-making processes. The Athenians granted citizenship rights to free men not born in Athens far more often than they granted citizenship to freed slaves, but nevertheless granted it rarely. They were prepared to concede the right to pay only the taxes that citizens paid and the right to own land rather more often than rights to citizenship itself. In their parsimony with citizenship they contrast markedly with the Romans, who granted citizenship on a large scale, first to the élites and then the entire free populations of the towns of Italy taken over by the expansion of Rome in the middle and late Republic, and then to the élites of the provinces of the empire, east and west. In the early third century AD citizenship was given to the entire freeborn population of the Roman empire. Athenian meanness with citizenship grants has to be seen once more in terms of maintaining the fiction that the citizen body was all alike: more or less eliminating the influx of outsiders, who might have grown up in a quite different society, ensured that the influx of ideas about how things might be done differently was also minimised.

It is in these terms too that we should think of the exclusion of women from political rights. There was a term *politis* that was the feminine form of *polites*, the term for citizen, but whereas a *polites* had rights to participation in the assembly and lawcourts, and to be elected or selected by lot as a magistrate, and obligations to serve in army or navy, a *politis* had no obligations. The only rights to participation which distinguished a *politis* from a free non-citizen were rights to participate in certain religious festivals and to take away a share of the sacrificial meat.

Exclusion of women from politics was universal in the Greek world, and Aristotle sought to explain this, too, in terms of nature: the male is more fitted to be in command than the female (*Politics* 1259a37–b10). Given the pattern of women marrying, shortly after puberty, men who, at around the age of thirty, might have been on a number of military campaigns and have spent a decade taking an active part in city politics, it can cause little surprise that women should seem so distinct from men. Similarly, given low life expectancy and the high number of births required of every mature woman to maintain the population, the pattern of women's life was necessarily very much contrasted to that of men. Exclusion of women from politics was essential to the fiction that all who participated could be considered to have enjoyed the same experiences.

Athenian life as it was enjoyed was equally dependent upon non-Greek slaves and upon Athenian women. Slaves formed the essential source of labour, and there seems to have been no threat to the supply of slaves. Getting a slave was a matter of purchasing power, and Athenians could assume that there were always more slaves to be had from the same sources as existing slaves had come from (in fact we hear amazingly little about the slave trade). Some slaves were bred at home, but many were bought when already adolescent. How long they then lived was to quite a large extent controlled by how well they were fed and how hard they were worked. Women were the essential source of future citizens, and the supply of Athenian women was strictly limited. Producing future generations of Athenian citizens depended upon the vagaries of human fertility and survival through the infant years when mortality was high and death visited almost at random.

For all that some slaves were made 'part of the family' in a very strong sense, and might be more closely involved in the nursing and education of Athenian children than the parents, slaves enjoyed a structural position in society quite different from that of women. In consequence, although slaves and women shared exclusion from politics, women played a central role in Athenian religious life, in which slaves had at best a marginal part. It is not by chance that, when Aristophanes contemplates women taking the law into their own hands in order to put an end to the war with Sparta, or to take action against what they see as misogynist plots in the plays of Euripides, he places those women's actions in a religious context. The action against Euripides is imagined as taking place at the women-only festival of Demeter, known as the Thesmophoria, which Aristophanes presents as taking the same form as a meeting of the Assembly. The action against war centres on the Athenian Acropolis, which the women occupy, led by one Lysistrata, whose name is likely to pun on the name of the woman who was then priestess of Athena, Lysimakhe.

Both these plays, *Lysistrata* and *Women at the Thesmophoria*, depend for their humour on the absurdity of the plots. The same is true of the later play, *Women at the Assembly*, in which Aristophanes imagines women disguising themselves, packing the Assembly, and voting for it to hand over the running of the city to the women. There was never any chance that women would in fact intervene on the political stage. But those plays, together with the suggestion in Plato's *Republic* that women might run the ideal city along with men, demonstrate that women's political role was at least thinkable, in a way that slaves running anything was not. When in Aristophanes the question comes up of who will do the work if the women run the state, the answer is: the slaves. Slavery was essentially a condition of subordination: when the swineherd Eumaios remarks in the *Odyssey* that the gods take away half a man's wits on the day on which he is enslaved (*Odyssey* 17.323), he is reflecting the impossibility of even the most cunning slave taking the initiative. Women's initiative, by contrast, was something that Athenian men were well familiar with; the same women who married men twice their age when themselves barely adult outlived their husbands and could expect to acquire considerable authority over the households of their children. When Lysias presents the case for Diogeiton having swindled his dead brother's children (Lysias 32), the listing of the property involved is presented through an imagined speech of the brother's widow. Aristotle in *Politics* builds up the city from its constituent households; just as women very clearly had a major stake in the household, so they had a stake too in the way in which the city was run.

Women's centrality to the city is reflected in their centrality in its religious life. There were in fact more festivals in Greek cities that excluded men – in particular festivals of Demeter, the goddess associated with human and plant fertility – than festivals that excluded women, though a few festivals of Heracles did exclude them. Defending the city against men depended on soldiers and sailors, and it was not thought appropriate that women should be either; defending it against the gods depended upon prayer and sacrifice, and in these areas the more people involved the more united the city could be seen to be in its thankfulness and its petitions. Women might be thought of as particularly dear to the gods: archaic inscriptions apply the epithet 'very beautiful object giving pleasure' very frequently to votive statues in the form of women, very rarely to votive statues in the form of men. The woman herself 'given in marriage' figured in sanctuaries as the very image of the gift. Women's lives and bodies were more obviously subject to divine intervention than men's, what with the vagaries not only of fertility but also of menstruation in a world of frequent malnutrition. No city could contemplate withdrawing women from its dialogue with the gods.

Nor was religion an occasional activity. Emphasis on the great religious festivals, whether those for all Greeks, such as the Olympic or Pythian games, or those for all members of a single city, like the Panathenaia at Athens, gives a misleading impression. Every sort of group within the Greek city had its own religious calendar, from the family, through the phratry, a (fictive) kinship group to which wives at least were certainly introduced, and the *genos* or descent group responsible for servicing a particular cult, to the deme. Calendars inscribed on stone show that demesmen might get together to sacrifice several times a month, and it is clear that both Athenian men and women could find themselves engaged in religious sacrifices on a more than weekly basis. Sacrifice was, indeed, the major source of meat in the diet. No doubt, not all who might do so did in fact participate in every sacrifice, but it is equally clear that the idea that women were 'let out of' the house to participate in religious cult activity only occasionally, and as a sort of 'safety valve', quite mistakes the importance of religion within the lives of free men and women. It was arguably the religious group, not the political group, that was the prime social group in the Greek city – for men as well as for women. After all, the Athenian Assembly met only forty times a year and at best could accommodate only 20 per cent of the eligible citizen body. Athens boasted more religious festivals than any other city: our image of Athenian democracy needs to be an image of both men and women queuing up for their share of roast or boiled mutton from sacrifice, not an image of Pericles haranguing a vast crowd from the speaker's stand in the Pnyx.

At the Panathenaia in the fifth century much of that meat was provided by Athens' Delian League allies. Athenian democracy did not depend upon the oppression of other Greek cities in the same way as it depended upon the oppression of slaves and women. Democracy continued in the fourth century even at periods when Athens could call on no material support from any allies. But the possession of an empire did play a very important part in what it was to be an Athenian in the latter two-thirds of the fifth century. Empire provided opportunities for enrichment to Athenians of all sorts – land abroad, gifts from grateful subjects, wages for military or civil service, wages for participation in state enterprises at home that would not have been undertaken but for the tribute income that Athens received. The subjects of the empire formed a group to which all Athenians could feel superior: they had obligations, military and financial as well as religious, but they had no possibility of acquiring rights at Athens. Formally independent, the foreign policy of allies was entirely constrained (those who tried to leave the Delian league were forced back into line by military action) and even their judicial freedom was curtailed as Athenians insisted on hearing capital trials themselves so that allies did not use their courts to kill off Athenian sympathisers. Pericles' funeral speech talks of Athens' special role in the education of Greece (Thucydides 2.41). For us the most striking lesson is that the lofty ideals of liberty advertised in that speech were achieved at the cost of systematic oppression.

Chapter 7

The unity and diversity of
the Greek city

The city of liberty and oppression was Athens. Athens dominates classical Greek history, not just because it dominated classical Greece, as it certainly did in the later fifth century but can hardly be said to have done in the fourth century, but because so much of the literature, art and archaeology that has come down to us was produced in Athens.

Of the great surviving fifth- and fourth-century historians, Herodotus was a native of Halikarnassos, a city with a very mixed and only part Greek population in south-west Anatolia, but both Thucydides and Xenophon were Athenians. Plenty of other cities produced men who wrote histories (the only woman recorded as having written histories is Thucydides' daughter, said to have been responsible for Thucydides Book 8), but none of their work survives in more than brief extracts, although some of those were very influential on later writers, particularly Ephoros from Kyme in Anatolia.

The situation is most extreme in the case of drama, where only plays by Athenian authors survive – Aeschylus, Sophocles, Euripides, Aristophanes, Menander. In philosophy relatively few Athenians seem to have been prominent, but not only were the only two major Athenian philosophers, Socrates and Plato, tremendously important, but the only other classical philosopher whose work survives extensively, Aristotle, although a native of Stageira in the north Aegean, worked mainly at Athens and established his 'school' there, at the Lyceum. Aristotle's *Poetics*, the first systematic work of literary criticism, was devoted to the analysis of tragedy and, though that book is now lost, comedy, and is dominated by examples drawn from Athenian literature.

In drama, history and philosophy Athens' predominance may be a result of its size; it is not obvious that it has anything to do with its democracy. In the case of Greek oratory, where again all surviving speeches were produced in Athens (although Lysias was a resident alien, a metic, not a citizen), the democracy itself is likely to have been an important factor. It was the democratic assembly and the use of popular courts that required the development of rhetorical skills, and although the art of rhetoric is associated with figures from Sicily, including the sophist Gorgias, it was in Athens that both the practice and the analysis of rhetoric became most developed: the first great treatise on rhetoric to survive, Aristotle's *Rhetoric*, is, once more, dominated by Athenian examples.

But just because Athens was dominant, we should not believe that it was typical. In many respects it was obviously exceptional: as we have seen, it was much larger than any other city in population, and it was larger than any apart from Sparta and Syracuse in the area of its territory. It was also, not least by virtue of the silver mines at Laureion, exceptionally rich. In consequence the Athenian economy was quite different from the economy of most other cities, in which the economic base was very largely agricultural. As we have already seen, even the consequences of Athens' silver mines for Athenian society were affected, one might almost say determined, by the Athenian constitution: it was Athens' democracy that made it inevitable that a non-citizen workforce be made to work the mines. Economy and politics are meshed closely together in the Greek city.

Major classical authors and their dates.
All are Athenian except where otherwise indicated

Aeschylus, tragedian c.525–456: fought at Marathon, earliest tragedy 499, first victory 484

Sophocles, tragedian c.495–406: Treasurer of Athena 443/2, General 441/0, *proboulos* 412, known to have been defeated by Aeschylus in 459, earliest known victory 447

Euripides, tragedian c.480–407/6: earliest tragedy 455, earliest victory 441

Herodotus of Halikarnassos, historian c.480–c.410

Socrates, philosopher 469–399: fought as a hoplite at Potidaia, Amphipolis, and Delion (424), *bouleutes* 405

Thucydides, historian c.455–c.400

Aristophanes, comic dramatist c.450–c.386: earliest comedy 427, first prize at Lenaia in 425 with *Acharnians*

Xenophon, historian c.430–355

Plato, philosopher c.429–347

Lysias, Athenian metic, forensic orator, c.430–380

Demosthenes, forensic and political orator 384–322

Aristotle of Stageira, philosopher 384–322

Menander, comic dramatist 344–292

Something of the variety of political arrangements in the Greek world has already been glimpsed. We have met tyranny in the classical as well as the archaic city, kingship in archaic and early classical Cyrene, the dual kingship at Sparta. We have met restrictions on political rights for those who ply their trade in the agora, that is, the restricted citizen body of an oligarchy. While his *Poetics* and *Rhetoric* are dominated by examples drawn from Athens, Aristotle's *Politics* draws its examples from all over the Greek world.

The city other than Athens about whose constitution and politics we know most is Sparta. But the study of Sparta is peculiarly difficult. This is because, following the loss of control of Messenia in the fourth century, in the third century BC Sparta reinvented itself. In the name of returning to the system of Lykourgos, the figure to whom Sparta's constitutional laws were ascribed in the classical period, a substantially new system of rigid citizen equality based on state allocation of land was imposed. Later authors' accounts of early Spartan history are contaminated with this later reinvention, and distinguishing what classical Sparta was like from what authors later than the third century considered it to be like is extremely difficult. It is made more difficult because classical Sparta was notorious for its secrecy, and in the absence of knowledge Athenians, in particular, invented a Sparta very much the opposite of their own society. We can see this very clearly in the contrasts between Athens and Sparta drawn by Thucydides himself and in the speeches which Thucydides ascribes to others. This phenomenon has sometimes been called the 'Spartan mirage', and it presents to the historian all the danger that mirages present to travellers in the desert.

In some ways Sparta was in fact very like Athens. At Sparta, too, the fiction that citizens were all alike – and Spartiates referred to themselves as *homoioi*, 'similars' – was maintained by ensuring that no citizen had to labour for another or engage in any menial activity. In the case of Sparta this was achieved through the exploitation of a subjugated population, not by the purchase and importation of non-Greek slaves. We do not know when, or how, the helots of Lakonia were subjugated, but, as we have seen, the helots of Messenia were reckoned to have been subjugated in the eighth century BC.

Helots differed from the chattel slaves found in Attica not only in their origin but in their relationship to their owners. Strabo's statement (8.5.4), written in the first century BC, that 'Spartans owned them as slaves who were, in a certain sense, public' may be a reflection of the third-century BC reforms, but even in the classical period helots were much more frequently the object of state intervention, without reference to their owners, than were slaves in Athens. Helots could, for example, be got rid of by the state. Thucydides (4.80) records that during the Peloponnesian War the Spartans asked for helot volunteers, expecting that the most rebellious helots would volunteer first, and that 2,000 who volunteered were never seen again. It was also claimed that part of what it was to grow up to be a Spartan citizen was to be sent out on missions secretly to kill helots. Unlike chattel slaves, helots had some sort of family life, and a helot family would farm a given plot of land for generations. Given that helots seem to have worked the land on a share-cropping system (Tyrtaios frg. 6W), there were good economic as well as social reasons for helots wanting to stay put and to reap the rewards of whatever good husbandry practices they had employed. Their Spartan masters shared the economic motivation for not moving them, and in any case discouraging helot movement had the advantage of keeping the lines of communication in the helot community weak.

Lines of communication in the slave community at Athens tended to be weak because the slaves were drawn from a variety of non-Greek origins, dulling their sense of similarity one to another and creating linguistic barriers to conspiracy. The helot community, in contrast, shared an origin and a language, and the Spartans were ever aware that revolt was a ready possibility. In the 460s, after an earthquake, the helots had actually revolted and it took a decade of military activity to restore peace (Thucydides 1.101–3). The organisation of helotage at Sparta was clearly rather different from the organisation of slavery at Athens, and the experience of being a helot was very different from the experience of being an Athenian chattel slave. But the construction of helots as an other against which the Spartiates defined themselves was but a more blatant form of the othering of slaves at Athens. We are told that in Sparta helots were made to dress in a different and degrading manner and were used to display, and hence warn Spartans off, human weaknesses.

When we ask how Sparta differed from Athens, economics and politics are found to be interwoven. Sparta had no mineral resources and the basis of its economy was agricultural. In Athens citizen and slave were contrasted in their differential roles in mining and domestic service, but they could and did work side by side in agriculture. In Sparta the distinction was made in agriculture, with Spartiates playing no part and helots entirely responsible. But the political organisation of agriculture had economic consequences. Helots farmed on a share-cropping system: they paid a certain amount to the Spartiate owner of the land, and kept the rest for themselves. There was a strong incentive for the helots to farm to a level of productivity sufficient to ensure that they themselves were always left comfortably provided for, but there was no incentive to maximise productivity since they were tied to the land and the only routes out of helot status seem to have been via military service or other services to the Spartan state. One consequence of this was that, whereas at Athens demands from the city for increased contributions from citizens could lead directly to more intensive exploitation of the land, in Sparta any pressure to greater productivity had to be indirect rather than direct. In economics as in politics, there was not much elasticity at Sparta.

Chattel slaves and helots had one further feature in common. Although they might be freed, that freedom did not confer any political rights. In Athens a freed slave gained the same status as the resident foreigner. In Sparta the freed helot seems similarly to have acquired a status that left him in a limbo, no longer ruled but not ruling either, but this was a limbo that was not just political but physical: Sparta seems not to have wanted freed helots around, and there is some evidence for their being settled in communities on the border of Spartan or Messenian territory (Thucydides 5.34.1). Moving from freed slave to citizen was rare in Athens and may have been rarer still at Sparta, although some sources do imply that in certain circumstances it was possible.

At Athens city decisions were taken in the citizen Assembly; at Sparta all the Spartiates together took fundamental decisions.

From that point of view Sparta can be described as a democracy. But there are also grounds for reckoning Sparta a monarchy or an oligarchy. Spartan kings were enormously influential figures. One king normally commanded the Spartans in war, and a king who was a good general, like Agesilaos who was king in the early part of the fourth century, became thereby a dominant figure in the politics of his day, not only in Sparta itself but among the allies who would seek to influence Spartan attitudes towards them through friendship with one or other of the kings. To some extent the power of the kings was a product of specific powers invested in them, including decisions regarding heiresses and property, but to a large extent kingly power was a matter of charisma. That charisma was important for persuading the Assembly – and on the vast majority of occasions of which we know the Assembly did indeed decide for a course of action advocated by a king. It was also important for dealing with the *Gerousia*, the council of elders. The powers of the *Gerousia* are not completely clear, but it is certain at least that they, along with the five chief magistrates, the ephors, who were elected annually, and the other king, constituted the court before which any king charged with an offence was tried. Partly because the two rival kings often adopted diametrically opposed policies, divided opinion among the Spartiate body, and could clash in public, trials of kings were not that infrequent, and the threat of trial itself influenced kingly behaviour. But it is conceivable that the *Gerousia* had more direct influence too, for there is some possibility that, like the Council of 500 at Athens, it predigested the business of the Assembly and made recommendations on what should be decided. But unlike the Council of 500, chosen by lot from citizens over the age of 30 according to a system of quotas for each deme, the *Gerousia* was a body of men over the age of 60, chosen by election.

Whatever we reckon the constitution of Sparta to have been, monarchy, oligarchy or democracy, there is no doubt that other Greeks saw Sparta and Athens as political opposites. One effect of this, as we have already seen, was to encourage civil discord in cities, as different groups matched pro-Athenian or pro-Spartan policies to preferences for different constitutional arrangements. Not surprisingly, perhaps, Sparta and Athens share the feature of having been politically very stable during the classical period, when we know other cities to have gone through a number of constitutional changes. But for all the propaganda advantages of advertising that one was like Athens or like Sparta in constitution, no other cities adopted the Spartan constitution, and even parallels with the Athenian pattern tend to be less than thoroughgoing. This is partly because a Spartan system required helots, and although there were subjugated populations in some other parts of the Greek world, for instance the *penestai* in Thessaly, a city that wished to imitate Sparta could not simply invent a subjugated population overnight. The Athenian system with its demes and tribes was designed to cope with a city with a very large population spread over a very large territory. Without those two factors being in play there was little need for such complexity.

Outside Athens and Sparta most of our information about constitutions comes from inscriptions, sometimes backed up by passing mentions in Aristotle or in the historians. The way in which cities record their decrees reveals the nature of magistracies, the presence or absence of a council, and so on. But there is some gap between having the institutions for democracy and operating a truly democratic system. The existence of a popular assembly does not mean that it was open to any citizen to speak at that assembly. Who was a citizen varied from city to city, as Aristotle makes clear in his discussion at the beginning of *Politics* Book 3. The existence of an assembly does not mean that all freeborn natives of the city were allowed to attend. And even if they were allowed to attend they might not be in a position to do so. The fact that Rhodes and Iasos instituted pay for attending the assembly, as did Athens in the fourth century, suggests that even in a small city economic factors might militate against some citizens in practice attending the assembly.

Different cities took different decisions about some fundamental political questions: what should the qualification be for citizenship? Should there be a council to take a preliminary look at business, and if so who should be on it? How many magistrates were needed, what should they be called, and should they be chosen by election or by lot? Sparta notoriously elected by acclamation (the loudest shout wins); Athens chose the vast majority of magistrates by lot but operated a complex system for electing generals from the ten tribes which normally resulted in one general from each tribe but could allow more than one from one tribe and none from another; the Boiotian cities operated a complicated system involving the rich serving on the council by rotation. But what is striking amid the diversity of answers to these fundamental questions is agreement on the questions. Cities might disagree whether to apply a property qualification to citizenship, or whether to exclude certain professions, but no city gave political rights to the under-eighteens, to women, to resident foreigners, or to slaves. Methods of election might vary, but, with the exception of hereditary kingship at Sparta, magistracies were not inherited and the first-born had no political privileges. For all the ideological disputes and the blood shed in civil strife, the terms of the disagreement were closely delimited.

This relates to a further issue. As we have already seen, politics and law were closely bound up together, and the agreement on the basic framework of constitutional issues goes together with an agreement on the basic framework of legal issues. But to what extent can we talk about 'Greek law' rather than 'Athenian law' or 'Spartan law'? On the one hand it is clear that individual laws were not the same everywhere. The rules regulating property ownership by women, for example, were not the same across the Greek world. Athenian women had very restricted property rights in their own person and inherited property only as a channel for it to be passed on to their children, but in some other cities, including Sparta, women could inherit property in their own right. But behind the variety of individual laws there are certain patterns: laws in different cities regularly take the same shape. We cannot fill the gaps in our knowledge of law in one city by bringing in laws from another city, but we can have some confidence that the sorts of matters regarded as appropriate for legislation and the sorts of terms in which laws were framed were substantially similar from city to city.

One area in which some general consonance between the laws of one city and the laws of another was important was in international law. The easy movement of individuals about the Greek world, and in particular the entering of an individual into contractual arrangements with individuals in another city, depended upon the possibility of parties to the contract being able to gain legal redress in the event of breach of contract. Such circumstances arose in the case not only of shipowners and merchants, but also of building contractors, and we have a number of building contracts which make specific provision for how disputes involving free non-citizens are to be settled. By the fifth century cities were making bilateral agreements with each other, known as *symbola*, a name derived from the physical objects that originally served as tallies to mark such agreements. *Symbola* guaranteed legal reciprocity. Some cities established special courts to try non-citizens, sometimes with a fast-track procedure to minimise inconvenience, and pairs of cities might make specific agreements about whose law was to apply in the case of disputes between their citizens.

But there was also another aspect to international law, and this was the relations between the cities themselves. The making of treaties is the other side of the making of wars, and numerous examples survive, some of them made to end a war, some of them made to prevent a war. But even in the absence of treaties there were recognised conventions as to what was and what was not acceptable in terms of behaviour to an enemy. Truces were expected to be kept, heralds to be respected and not harmed, and those who surrendered were expected not to be harmed. These were only conventions, and exceptions are not infrequently found, particularly with regard to the treatment of captives. Cities that breached the conventions, however, were liable to be ill-regarded and might themselves suffer in consequence.

In the opening action of the Peloponnesian War in 431 BC, the Thebans attempted, but failed, to take Plataia, and 180 of them were captured and then executed by the Plataians (Thucydides

2.4–6). The Thebans complained that this was contrary to an agreement that the captives should be handed back in turn for a Theban withdrawal. Four years later, when Plataia had been besieged, and eventually captured, by the Thebans and Spartans, the Thebans brought up the 'illegal' killing as a reason for not showing mercy to the Plataians. No mercy was shown and they were executed, to the number of 200 (Thucydides 3.66, 68). The terms of the debate here suggest that killing prisoners in breach of an oath was distinctly less acceptable than killing them would have been had there been no oath.

On a number of other occasions prisoners are killed simply for convenience, and the arguments against doing this are largely that it gives a bad impression. This is the case with the Spartan Alkidas, who arrives too late to help Mytilene revolt against Athens and whose killing of prisoners taken during his voyage leads to a warning that such behaviour does not fit with a rhetoric of liberation (Thucydides 3.29–32). Keeping prisoners alive gave a bargaining tool. This is seen in the role of the Spartans captured by the Athenians on the island of Sphakteria in 424; Spartan anxiety about the fate of these men was a significant factor in bringing about the peace treaty of 421 known as the Peace of Nicias. There was a similar logic to the Corcyrean behaviour in 434 when, after winning a battle against the Corinthians, they slaughtered all their captives except the Corinthians themselves (Thucydides 1.30.1). A sequel to this episode reveals the dangers in behaving differently. When the Corinthians achieved a naval victory over Corcyra in 433, they made no attempt to capture prisoners from the disabled ships, but instead butchered them. In the process they butchered their own friends too (Thucydides 1.50.1).

Much more respect was shown to the dead than to those captured alive. The plot of Sophocles' *Antigone* turns on Creon's refusal of burial to Polyneikes, who has made war on his native city. Euripides in *Suppliants* has Theseus claim that no man would be brave were he not sure of burial for his body (538–41), and Isokrates explicitly compares the fate of living and dead, saying that to ignore the burial of the dead is worse for those failing to bury them while being deprived of a city is the worst fate for victims (14 *Plataicus* 55). Seeing to the burial of the dead was one of the prime tasks of a victorious general, and defeated generals were expected to make a truce in order to recover the war dead. Only in extreme circumstances did a general fail to do so, as after the massive slaughter of Ambrakiots in two successive days of fighting in 426/5 (Thucydides 3.109.1–2, 113). When the Athenian generals who won the naval battle of Arginousai in the last years of the Peloponnesian War failed see that either the living or the dead were picked up because of a storm, they were quite exceptionally (and unconstitutionally) put on trial as a body by the Assembly and all who appeared at the trial were executed (Diodoros 13.100.1 for the dead being at issue as well as the living, on whom Xenophon *Hellenica* 1.6.35ff. concentrates).

Observing an oath and burying the dead could both be regarded as a religious duty. Although burial was not a religious ceremony in ancient Greece, in so far as no religious personnel were required to be present, the gods could be represented as expected to take vengeance on those who denied burial. But the dead themselves could be thought to be powerful. We have already met the dead as a source of knowledge, as Periander is held to have sought information from his dead wife Melissa through necromancy, or as Odysseus in *Odyssey* 11 summons up ghosts to inform him about both past and future. But they could also be a source of intervention, either on their own behalf or on behalf of others. The Erinyes who seek Orestes' blood for the murder of Clytemnestra his mother are one fictional example of this. We have inscribed sacred laws from Selinous in Sicily in the fifth century and Cyrene in Libya in the fourth century, both of which deal with how to cope with avenging spirits. These examples come from the fringes of the Greek world, but even in classical Athens we find curse tablets deposited in the graves of the dead, perhaps particularly of those who had died untimely deaths. These curses regularly take the form of wishing that the person cursed become like the dead person – powerless, unable to act, whether it be to act in court or to act in love or in business.

Alongside this universal Greek respect for the body of the dead and fear of the power of the dead went an apparent indifference to how the body of the dead person was dealt with. We have already seen that at Pithekoussai in the eighth century both cremation and inhumation rites were used, and although some Greek cities at some periods predominantly used one rite, and others another, some cities, such as Athens, not infrequently practised both rites at the same time. This is despite the fact that the story about Periander claims that clothes need to be burnt in order to be available to Melissa and that curse tablets seem only to be found in inhumations, not cremations.

Greek cities were very far from being uniform in the nature of their religious rituals. Although sanctuaries with temples housing images of gods were universal, the form of the temples varied from place to place, as did the placing of the most important sanctuary with regard to the centre of population. In Athens there were important 'out-of-town' sanctuaries, such as the sanctuary of Demeter and Kore at Eleusis, the home of the Eleusinian Mysteries, or the sanctuary of Poseidon at Sounion. But there can be no doubt that it was the festivals centred on the Athenian Acropolis itself that were most prominent in the life of the city. Elsewhere the most important sanctuary might be well outside the main town, like the sanctuaries of Hera at Argos and Samos. The Argive Heraion was some eight miles from Argos town, the Samian Heraion almost as far from the town on Samos. That out-of-town sanctuaries might be conceptually central is itself a mark of the way in which the countryside was integral to what it was to be a Greek polis, and the emergence of such sanctuaries in the eighth century has been seen as an important mark of the 'birth of the polis'. But the different placing of the gods in different cities, and indeed at different times in the same city, for some sanctuaries waxed and waned in popularity, is one indicator of how different it might be to live in different cities.

If differences in the placing of sanctuaries are what most obviously differentiates cities religiously 'on the map', there were other major differences on site. Different sanctuaries attracted different sorts of buildings and different sorts of dedication. The hexastyle peripteral temple which we tend to think of as the 'standard' Greek temple was a widespread feature, but it was by no means universal. The sanctuary at Eleusis had a massive 'Telesterion' where the Mysteries took place, but no 'standard' temple. The needs of the Eleusinian cult were quite different from the needs of most other cults, in so far as initiates needed a room within which to gather, whereas the rooms of temples housed statues of and offerings to the deity, but not the worshippers. At other sites the temple building itself was small, and other buildings were more dominant. At the sanctuary of the hero Amphiaraos at Oropos, to which people went for healing, the most imposing buildings were the theatre and the stoa in which the sick slept overnight and were visited and cured by the god. At the Kabirion near Thebes, where the rather mysterious 'Kabiroi' were worshipped, the central feature was a theatre.

Contrasts in dedications were even more marked. In the sixth century some sanctuaries attracted dedications in the form of *kouroi*, statues of naked young men in a stiff upright posture, or *korai*, similar upright statues of clothed maidens. Surviving statues and fragments suggest that there were more than a hundred *kouroi* at the sanctuary of Apollo on Mount Ptoion near Akraiphnion in Boiotia. A very large number of *korai* were found in the excavations of the Athenian Acropolis in the nineteenth century, after they had been dumped in a pit following the Persian sack of Athens in 480. At the Heraion on Samos both monumental *kouroi* and *korai* were dedicated. But many Greek sanctuaries have yielded no trace of *kouros* dedications, including such major sanctuaries as that of Zeus at Olympia or Hera at Argos. Such contrasts in dedications are also found when it comes to smaller dedications. Two sanctuaries have been excavated at Emborio on Chios, one on the acropolis on whose slopes the archaic settlement clustered, and the other down by the harbour. Both sanctuaries were in use simultaneously, but the harbour sanctuary attracts exotic dedications, including such things as jewellery and oriental bronze belts, while the acropolis sanctuary attracts dedications which seem more closely related to civic life, including votive shields.

Temple plans and dedications are some of the outward and visible signs of the variety of cult practices. There is no doubt that the variety was mirrored in what went on. Surviving 'sacred laws' (that is temple regulations) and cult calendars indicate variations, both from sanctuary to sanctuary and from festival to festival, in who could participate (we have already met cults which exclude men and cults which exclude women), what was sacrificed (different animals get sacrificed to different deities, e.g. pigs to Demeter, goats to Artemis), whether the meat could or could not be taken out of the sanctuary, whether libations were in wine or not, and so on. They also reveal local concerns about decorum. There seems to have been particular concern about how women dressed in some Peloponnesian sanctuaries, for instance, and explicit articulation of concerns about sexual purity or menstruating women comes largely in the hellenistic period. One of our earliest sacred laws, from Olympia, appears to forbid sexual intercourse in the sanctuary, but the plot of one of Menander's comedies turns on a girl having been 'raped' during an all-night festival of the virgin goddess Artemis at Halai Araphenides in eastern Attica.

For all the continued variety, there is no doubt that Greek cities became culturally more similar to one another over time. We see this in the alphabet. In the archaic period very large numbers of local scripts can be distinguished, several of them using letters which we would not immediately recognise as Greek (qoppa, digamma, san, etc.), as well as writing the letters we are familiar with in unfamiliar ways. The Athenians simply did not have the letters omega or eta or xi or psi in their archaic script. But the Athenians went over to the Ionic alphabet at the end of the fifth century and scripts became standardised. Those standardised ways of writing coexisted with dialectal differences in the language spoken and written, but in the hellenistic period those too faded out as a 'common language', *koine*, was adopted. In pottery too, regional styles can be relatively easily distinguished in the Geometric pottery of the eighth century, and still in the seventh century a large number of cities produced distinctive fine pottery, although the quantity of pottery produced in Corinth was far larger than that produced anywhere else. But in the sixth century Athenian pottery began to dominate the fine pottery market, both on the Greek mainland and elsewhere, and during the fifth century only negligible quantities of fine decorated pottery are made in any part of mainland Greece or the islands other than Athens. In sculpture regional styles of *kouros* and *kore* can be distinguished in the sixth century; within classical sculpture there are some regional specialities, but in so far as styles can be distinguished the distinctions are of workshop rather than region.

Developments that start in one place get adopted all over the Greek world. That must have been true of the highly artificial conventions of the Doric and Ionic orders of architecture developed around 600 BC, but it is notably true with tragedy. For all that we talk of 'Greek tragedy', tragedy was an Athenian development and all surviving plays were written by Athenians. But already in the fifth century Aeschylus was taking plays to Sicily and Euripides writing in Macedonia, and the massive spread of theatres throughout the classical Greek world is something of a measure of the diffusion of tragedy – and indeed, somewhat more surprisingly, of often highly topical Athenian comedy.

It was, of course, with Athenian dominance that we began. That Athens dominates surviving literature and archaeology is not random, but reflects the way in which Athenian products came to dominate in the Greek world. That dominance is not independent of Athens' size. Athens' size, and in the fifth and fourth centuries its local wealth in the form of Laureion silver, created a market that made it well worth Greeks from elsewhere visiting. It also created demands, for example for food, that ensured that merchants would always be looking for Athenian goods, as well as Athenian silver, to carry as return cargoes. Market forces may have stimulated the production of quality pottery in Athens. Political forces in the fifth century created a will to excel and to prove the truth of the claim to be an education to Greece. But the very attraction of Greeks and others from elsewhere to Athens itself acted as a stimulus, and Athens' cultural centrality long outlasted its defeat, and the halving of its citizen population, in the Peloponnesian War. But what happened after that war is the subject of the last chapter.

Chapter 8

Was Alexander the end of Greek history?

The defeat of Athens by Sparta in the Peloponnesian War brought an end to the Athenian empire. But it did not bring a general backlash against democracy. Spartan behaviour saw to that. The problems with Spartan supremacy emerge from the events at Athens itself. There Lysander, the Spartan general most responsible for Sparta's military victories, not only saw to the surrender of the city and the pulling down of its defences, but lent his support to a small group of Athenians who installed themselves as a violent junta, the so-called 'Thirty Tyrants'. The Thirty were united by dislike for radical democracy rather than by shared positive ideals. They engaged in wanton violence against those who could be presented as public enemies – wealthy non-Athenians resident at Athens, such as the father of the orator Lysias, and Athenians whose activities as prosecutors in court had made them unpopular. But the Thirty became split over just how narrowly or broadly based their régime should be, and the hard core of the junta maintained their power only by bringing over to their side, by bribes and other buttering up, Kallibios, the commander of the Spartan garrison which they had procured (Plutarch *Lysander* 15.5).

The behaviour of the Thirty provoked a mass movement to restore democracy. Those who fled from the Thirty were harboured by the Boiotians, despite an express Spartan order to their allies to the contrary. A core of Athenian opponents of the Thirty gathered at the border fort of Phyle and marched on Athens, gathering further support as they came. A battle was fought in the Piraeus in which Kritias, the hardline leader of the Thirty, was killed. The Spartan king Pausanias, who had been sent to Athens to deal with the situation, initially opposed the rising against the Thirty, but he then chose to move his support to the returning democrats and the Thirty collapsed. Democracy was restored, and the Spartans departed. Pausanias was brought to trial in Sparta and acquitted by a narrow margin because, although the members of the *Gerousia* were equally split, he managed to command the support of all five ephors elected for that year (Pausanias 3.5.1–2).

The events at Athens bring out clearly the problems with Spartan imperialism. Sparta was interested in control, and sought to control other states by having its 'friends' in power (Plutarch *Lysander* 13.2–5). Without any ideological commitment to any particular set of constitutional principles (aristocracy of birth, plutocracy, meritocracy, or whatever) no quality control was exercised over the choice of friends. Furthermore, Sparta exercised no control over how those friends acted: loyalty and friendship were the only qualities demanded, and if these were forthcoming the Spartans were prepared to back behaviour of all sorts with brute force that was often delivered by Spartans who themselves acted in a violent and capricious way. As if this was not bad enough, Sparta also acted inconsistently. Being friends with Sparta meant being friends with individual Spartans, but individual Spartans who had their own particular friends in power in too many places could themselves fall under suspicion. That seems to be what happened in the case of Lysander. It was he who had prosecuted the final phase of the war against Athens, and he who had been the Spartan on site with whom power-greedy locals were in a position to make friends. But when he returned to Sparta, fellow Spartans, and not least Pausanias, one of the two kings and never a champion of an aggressive Spartan foreign policy, resented his network of friends and were more than happy to undermine it. A decade later Pausanias lost out in another internal dispute and was exiled (Xenophon *Hellenica* 3.5.25); in the wake of that life became as problematic for his friends, for example at Mantineia in the 380s, as it had been for Lysander's friends in 403 (Xenophon *Hellenica* 5.2.3).

The way Sparta worked in the last years of the Peloponnesian War and in its aftermath was not in fact very different from the way in which Sparta had always acted. Sparta's old allies were, by the end of the Peloponnesian War, already distinctly suspicious of Sparta. The Thebans are said to have wanted to have Attica turned into a sheep pasture – not a sign of undying hostility to Athens but of fear of what might happen if the human and silver resources of Attica came into the Spartan pocket. Spartans had shown themselves repeatedly during the war to be ineffective in protecting their friends and harsh and unprincipled in their conduct abroad. We see this, for instance, in the history of the settlement at Herakleia in Trachis which the Spartans established in 426. The Spartans were invited in by the Trachinians after the Trachinians had suffered heavily in war at the hands of their neighbours the Oitaians. The Spartans insisted on allowing neither Ionians nor Achaians to take part in the settlement and then, in the words of Thucydides, 'did their full share of ruining its prosperity and reducing its population by governing harshly and in some cases unfairly and so frightening the great part of the population away' (3.93.2). Later, in his account of 419, Thucydides tells of the defeat of the new population of Herakleia at the hands of the Thessalians, who were not unnaturally annoyed at this new city on their borders, and of the subsequent occupation of the city by the Boiotians, who were afraid that Sparta's failure to protect the city would allow the Athenians to take it over. Among their other actions, the Boiotians sent away the Spartan Agesippidas for misgovernment (5.51–2). Typically, the story at Herakleia does not change much after the war. According to Diodoros, in 399 the Spartans intervened in Herakleia because there was civil strife there: the Spartan sent in to sort matters out simply executed, without trial, the 500 people whom he took to have been the cause of the trouble (Diodoros 14.38.4–5).

If its allies were suspicious of it, Sparta was similarly suspicious of some of its allies. Once free of the need to deal with Athens, the Spartans turned directly to administer discipline on allies whom they believed to have been less than loyal, and in particular Elis. The Spartans held a grudge against the Eleans for excluding Spartans from the Olympic games at one period during the war (Thucydides 5.49), allying with Athens, Argos and Mantineia (Thucydides 5.47) during the brief period when Sparta and Athens were not at war, following the Peace of Nicias (421–418), and refusing to allow King Agis to sacrifice to Zeus at Olympia for victory over the Athenians. The Spartans invaded Elis within five years of the end of the Peloponnesian War and insisted on splitting Elis up, making the Eleans give independence to the cities of Triphylia, the southern part of their territory (Xenophon *Hellenica* 3.2.21–31; cf. Diodoros 14.17.4–12; 14.34.1). Dividing up actually or potentially recalcitrant allies was, along with ruling through 'friends', a mark of Spartan 'imperialism', as it may reasonably be called. Not surprisingly, Sparta's most powerful allies, the Boiotians, again, and the Corinthians, refused to take part in the campaign against Elis.

The end of war with Athens freed up the Spartans to intervene over a much wider area. They got themselves involved, for instance, in fighting the Persians in Asia Minor. But there was hardly a theatre in which they intervened where they did not leave a foul reputation (cf. Xenophon *Hellenica* 3.1.8). Within a decade of the end of the Peloponnesian War Greece was plunged back into general war, admittedly of a somewhat desultory kind, as the Boiotians, Corinthians and Athenians got together to resist Sparta in the so-called Corinthian War. Within three decades of the end of the Peloponnesian War the Athenians were forming a new alliance with many of the cities that had been part of their fifth-century empire, under the slogan of ensuring that the Spartans leave the Greeks free and autonomous and able to live in peace. The Athenians made an undertaking to their old allies that this time there would be no garrisons, no Athenian landholding abroad, and no tribute: on those conditions many members of the fifth-century empire were prepared to sign up to this new league, sometimes termed 'The Second Athenian Confederacy'. Looking back, these cities clearly believed that being under Athens had been better than facing the prospect of arbitrary intervention from Sparta. Some of them may have decided, indeed, that being under Athens was better than going it alone in any circumstances. Athens offered protection not only from outside intervention but also from the subversion of democratic régimes: the Athenians too had their friends, but the friends were 'the demos' in general, and anyone who forwarded its interests, rather than particular individuals.

Athens was not the only beneficiary of Spartan caprice and heavy-handedness. Immediately to Athens' north were a series of cities which all identified themselves as Boiotian, but which were sufficiently unequal in power and resources to make any formal confederacy that they might form fragile. In the middle of the fifth century the active threat from Athens, which had exercised at least a loose overlordship over all the cities of Boiotia in the decade following the battle of Oinophyta in 456, brought about a formal confederacy. This confederacy had a formal constitution which guaranteed each member a political say in proportion to the number of troops that it supplied. But quickly the confederacy was turned into a Theban hegemony. The Theban attack on Plataia, which proved to be the opening event of the Peloponnesian War, resulted in the Thebans taking over the Plataian seats on the central council. Then Thebes took advantage of its military victory over Athens in the battle of Delion in 424 to suppress the neighbouring city of Thespiai, on the grounds that it was 'atticizing'. In the 380s, worried by the power exercised by a Thebes which was now its enemy, Sparta tried to insist on treating the cities of Boiotia as separate political units and not as a single unit, but its attempts to enforce this backfired. Sparta's repeated invasions of Theban territory and its opportunist occupation of the acropolis of Thebes, known as the Kadmeia, in 382 strengthened rather than weakened Thebes' hand in Boiotia. It also caused Thebes to develop a hoplite fighting force marked by a quite new professionalism.

In 371 that Theban army, commanded by a general named Epaminondas, who was one of the few to 'think outside the box' about how he used his troops, faced the Spartan army at Leuktra in western Boiotia. The Thebans achieved a crushing victory. To explain the site of the battle Plutarch tells a story about a previous incident of the rape and murder of girls by two Spartan soldiers and the refusal of the Spartan authorities to show any interest in punishing this crime (Plutarch *Love Stories* 3 [*Moralia* 773B–774D]). Although fictional, this story well reveals the strong sense that Spartan behaviour was bound to bring retribution, and this is also clearly reflected in the writings of the generally pro-Spartan and anti-Theban Xenophon.

Epaminondas was as good at seeing what needed to be done in the aftermath of victory as he was at delivering the victory in the first place. The Peloponnese was invaded, Messenia liberated and new cities built both in Messenia (Messene at the foot of Mount Ithome) and in Arkadia (Megalopolis, the Great City). The loss of Messenia dramatically reduced the agricultural resources available to the Spartans. The foundation of the new cities ensured that any attempt by the Spartans to recapture the territory lost could and would be effectively resisted. The walls of Messenia, built according to a state-of-the-art plan which was to be obsolete within twenty years, still stand as a monument to the determination that Sparta would never again be a major power.

If Sparta's dominance of the Greek world was short-lived, Theban dominance was shorter. Thebes was not well placed to exercise leadership. Although it made a short-lived attempt to man a navy, this was a doomed exercise: Thebes' territory had no major ports and from many parts of Boiotia access to the sea was difficult. Within Boiotia itself Theban supremacy was far from being universally welcomed. In each of the cities of Boiotia groups could be found who wanted to be rid of Theban hegemony, and Thebes maintained its position only by repressive action. Even within the city there was much in-fighting. Some of this was personal – resentment at the success of Epaminondas. But much of it seems to have been a matter of disagreements over fundamental policies: the Thebans acquired a reputation for meetings of their assembly going on for a very long time and being extremely volatile. One way and another, when Epaminondas was killed in the battle of Mantineia in 362, fighting against the now combined forces of Sparta and Athens, Thebes' decade as the most powerful of Greek cities effectively ended. Xenophon ended his account of Greek history, which he began at the point at which Thucydides Book 8 breaks off, with the battle of Mantineia. In one of the great closing sentences of all works of history he declares that he gives up at this point and leaves it to someone else since from that point on things were even more complicated than before (Xenophon *Hellenica* 7.5.27). That he gives up ensures that for us things are not only more complicated but also more obscure: the political history of the rest of the fourth century has to be pieced together from tendentious contemporary political speeches in Athens and from the writings of historians working very much later. Nevertheless, at least the outline of events is clear.

In retrospect the activities of the Thebans in the 370s and 360s not only mark an end, an end of Greek history focusing on struggle between Athens and Sparta, but also a beginning – the beginning of northern Greek involvement with the cities of southern Greece. Thebes had become drawn into conflict in the north as well as in the south, with Thessaly and Macedonia as well as with Sparta and Athens. Those activities caused one Philip, a member of the Macedonian royal house, to be for a period a hostage in Thebes (probably in the years 369–397). While there he observed Epaminondas' military innovations. When in 360/59 his brother, King Perdikkas III, was killed in a border war with the Illyrians to the north-west, Philip took power in Macedon and proceeded to apply the lessons which he had learned.

Philip's early reign saw hectic military activity on a number of fronts, but also army reforms. Philip turned the Macedonian army into something completely different from earlier Greek city-state armies, as his opponents came eventually to recognise. For a start Philip's army was a standing force able to fight at any time of year. Second, it was armed with much longer spears than had been usual, and these longer spears, known as sarissas, enabled Philip to pile his troops up very deep on parts of the line in order to force a break in the opponent's line, and to ensure that even troops well back in the ranks were able to contribute directly to warding off the enemy. Third, Philip made no concessions to gentlemanly behaviour in warfare. If he desired to capture a city he would use any means at his disposal to do so. He took over from the fourth-century tyrants of Sicily two ideas: using artillery, devices for shooting arrows, stones, etc., further than a single man or bow could shoot them, and using siege towers. Philip developed the torsion catapult, which came to be able to shoot a bolt over 300 m, though he himself used them only to shoot arrows. Suddenly, what a city needed in the way of defences was changed from a wall so long that the enemy could not possibly build a counter-wall round it (which is the way the defences of Messene were constructed), to a wall so strong that it could not be shot or battered down. In addition Philip was prepared to use the very considerable monetary resources at his disposal, especially after he secured the mines close to Krenides, which he refounded as Philippi. It became notorious that Philip could bribe his way into practically any town.

By the end of the 350s it was becoming apparent to politicians in Athens that Philip posed a serious long-term threat to their autonomy. In Athens there were many years of contentious debate between those, led by Demosthenes, who thought that Philip needed combating at all costs, and those, including Aischines, who thought that it was possible to find a way of peacefully cohabiting with him. The peace named after the Athenian politician Philokrates, which was made in 346, did not last, and Philip delivered a decisive blow to the freedom of the city-states with a victory at Chaironeia in Boiotia in 337, in which his son Alexander played a significant part. After that victory Philip imposed his own conditions on the whole Greek mainland, making a treaty with all significant cities except Sparta, the so-called 'League of Corinth'. This treaty obliged the Greek cities to provide soldiers for Philip's campaigns, but it did not, contrary to what had been feared at Athens, interfere with the constitutions of the individual cities.

Philip's willingness to leave the Greek cities largely alone was occasioned by his interests being elsewhere. During the 340s he had pursued his conquests east to the Propontis, a siege at Perinthos being one of his few unsuccessful endeavours. There is little doubt that he had already conceived larger ambitions: the Persians sensed a threat and sent help to Perinthos. Now, after Chaironeia, Philip sent two of his most trusted generals, Attalos and Parmenio, to begin the liberation of the Greek cities of Anatolia from Persia. A new enterprise had been conceived. But the man who conceived it was not to see it through. Philip's private life caught up with him.

Although Macedonians were accepted as Greek, after some discussion, for the purposes of competing at the Olympic games, and although the language of the Macedonians appears most probably to have been a dialect of Greek related to the dialects of north-west Greek, some Macedonian customs were distinct. One of these was polygamy. Philip married at least seven women, having several wives at the same time and not distinguishing between them in status. These multiple marriages were at least in part political. One wife was an Illyrian, married in the wake of settling problems on the Illyrian border, one was a Thessalian, one a Molossian, one a Thracian. But the politics of such unions was not limited to foreign policy. When Philip married again in 337 one Kleopatra, who came from a distinguished lowland Macedonian family, this was taken by some to signal that he favoured one part of his kingdom over another. When Philip appeared to condone some bad behaviour by Kleopatra's uncle towards a man from an outlying district of Macedonia, the man moved in and assassinated Philip at a theatrical performance that was part of the celebrations for another diplomatic marriage, that of one of his daughters to her uncle, the king of Epiros.

Philip's heir was his twenty-year-old son, Alexander. The accession of so young a man, and in circumstances liable to lead to internal division within Macedonia, offered a good chance to break free of Macedonian overlordship, and Alexander faced trouble from Thracians in the east, Paionians and Illyrians in the west, and from Greeks. Thebes revolted. In all cases Alexander acted swiftly and decisively. Alexander captured and razed the town of Thebes amid scenes of extreme violence: Greeks from neighbouring cities that had been oppressed by the Thebans joined in the slaughter and according to Diodoros (17.14.1) over 6,000 Thebans perished and more than 30,000 were captured. It was said that only the house of the poet Pindar was left standing, and that by the express order of Alexander.

Just as Philip had been keen to make peace with the Greek cities in order to turn his attentions to the east, so Alexander did likewise. In 334/3 he crossed into Asia. Neither he nor many of the Macedonian soldiers he took with him were ever to return. His progress east was rapid, but costly. In 334 he defeated a Persian army at the river Granikos. After liberating the Greek cities of Ionia and setting up some democratic regimes there he proceeded east, and in 333 again defeated the Persians, this time commanded by their king, Darius, at the river Issos. Sieges at Tyre and Gaza and the setting up of a new city, Alexandria in Egypt, consumed the next two years, but in 331 he decisively defeated Darius again, at Gaugamela. Babylon surrendered and Alexander now had the Persian empire and its capitals at Sousa and Persepolis under his control. After Granikos Alexander had already sent back spoils to the Athenian Acropolis, to mark his taking revenge on the Persians who had sacked Athens, and when he took Sousa he sent back to Athens the statues of the tyrannicides who had assassinated Peisistratos' son Hipparchos, statues which Xerxes had taken in 480 (Arrian *Anabasis* 3.18.7–8).

A campaign which had advertised itself as a campaign of revenge and of liberation for the Greeks could happily have ended here, but Alexander had other ideas. He continued east not only through the eastern part of the Persian empire, but beyond. In 327 he invaded India. The going was tough. Alexander became harsh and his men unhappy. He achieved a massive victory at the river Hydaspes, and slaughtered the enemy on a scale quite unlike that of the earlier defeats of the Persians. But when he reached the river Hyphasis his men would go no further. Alexander was forced to turn back, only to lose many men in a gruelling march through the Gedrosian desert. Morale was low and relations between Alexander and his men bad. Weary as they were with war, when Alexander announced that he was dismissing his veterans and enlisting fresh troops the veterans mutinied again, only to capitulate when Alexander turned to Persians to serve for him. It is a matter of much dispute whether Alexander believed in principle in treating all subjects of his new empire alike and deliberately mixed up Persian ways with Greco-Macedonian ways, and Persians with Greeks and Macedonians, for that reason, or whether such mixing was short-term expediency. Alexander's long-term plan was never to be revealed: he died, after heavy drinking, at Babylon in 323, just short of his 33rd birthday.

The history of the fifth century is generally written in terms of what the Spartans did and what the Athenians did, what the Corinthians did, and so on. Although Plutarch in antiquity found material to write lives of Themistocles, Aristeides, Kimon, Pericles, Nicias and Alcibiades, few historians in recent times have ventured to structure their fifth-century history even around Pericles, for all that the middle of the fifth century is sometimes called the 'Periclean Age'. The history of the early part of the fourth century can be similarly written as a history of Spartans and Athenians, of Corinthians and Thebans, but it is hard to understand what the Spartans did in these years without taking some account of the long reign of Agesilaos, and impossible to contemplate the brief Theban hegemony without reference to the strategic and tactical skills of Epaminondas. Already in the

390s Athens had established a new precedent by erecting, during his lifetime, an honorific statue of the general Konon, and from 360 onwards the fourth-century narrative is dominated by individuals, by Philip and Alexander, by Demosthenes, Aeschines and Lykourgos.

This is not merely a chance matter. The Persian Wars left Greek cities with tremendous self-confidence. It was not merely that Greeks had proved superior to Persians in battle, but that the various decisions which the Greeks had taken, both in their individual cities and when the various city commanders got together to discuss common moves, had proved to be the right decisions. Even traditions that Themistocles had got his way as much by trickery as by reasoned argument did not undermine the ensuing confidence in the corporate body. The detailed records of some assembly decisions at Athens provided by the decrees inscribed on stone show that individual Athenians whose names never make it into the neon lights of Aristophanes' comic satire or Thucydides' account of the Peloponnesian War did, nevertheless, attend, speak at, and persuade the Athenian Assembly. Famously, the decision taken in Sparta in 432 to go to war with Athens was a decision supported by neither of the Spartan kings: even at Sparta the collective body liberated itself from the authority of those hereditary leaders to obey the urgings of a newly elected ephor, Sthenelaidas, a man whose name appropriately must mean something like 'Strength of the People', and who has no further part in the historical narrative as we know it.

The Peloponnesian War destroyed that self-confidence. At Athens disillusion with the decisions which had led first to defeat in Sicily in 413 and then to final subjugation by Sparta played a major part in allowing democracy to be twice overthrown, in 411 and 404. In other cities, too, looking for a strong leader was one factor occasioning increased factionalism – as at Thebes in the 390s or in the Arkadia of the 360s. In Syracuse defeating Athens did not strengthen democracy but led rapidly to its overthrow and to the tyranny of Dionysios I. Writers in the fifth century saw virtue as well as folly in democratic decision-making. This is true of opponents of democracy, like the person, sometimes known as the Old Oligarch, responsible for the *Constitution of the Athenians* preserved with the works of Xenophon. It is true too of Thucydides, who for all his accounts of democratic failings nevertheless consistently suggests that a city which works together as a unit is stronger than one where the citizen body is divided. Writers in the fourth century expound theoretical positions supportive of democracy only to try to undermine them. Thus Plato quotes Protagoras' defence of democracy only to have Socrates argue him down, and in *Menexenus* he quotes a funeral speech, which he has Socrates ascribe to Pericles' mistress Aspasia, only to parody the absurdities of democratic self-deception that it displays. Plato himself seems to have seen most promise not in democracy but in the tyrants of Syracuse – though he was quite quickly disillusioned.

The success of Philip and Alexander might seem to prove the superiority of monarchy as a decision-making structure over democracy, and modern scholars have often talked of 'the crisis of the polis' or of the polis as 'doomed to extinction'. It is certainly true that Athens was hopeless at getting its act together against Philip, seeing the problem too late and not letting Demosthenes persuade it into decisive action. But such a conclusion oversimplifies the situation. What is at issue with Philip and Alexander, as to some extent earlier with Thebes, is the ability to get together resources of manpower and money on a scale far exceeding that of the individual city. In the fifth century Athens had managed something similar, but only by acting, as the Athenians themselves realised, like a tyrant among cities rather than by setting up any inter-polis democratic mechanism. Thebes similarly ended up lording it over its confederates as a tyrant, for all the constitutional rules according to which they were supposed to operate. Nor did confederacies elsewhere, for instance in Arkadia, fare much better in the fourth century. Philip and Alexander did not even have to pretend to constitutional rule – though that does not mean there were no rules of behaviour for them: as we have seen there were enough tensions within

Macedonia for Philip to be assassinated for the unwise actions of a close associate.

The history of Macedonia before Philip is a history of infighting, failure to pursue a consistent policy, and generally of weakness. The history of the successors of Alexander is a history of the immediate break-up of his empire between different dynasts who proceed to fight against each other over their shares. This background and this foreground leave little doubt that Philip and Alexander must be seen not as individuals who just happened to be in the right place at the right time, but as individuals of exceptional qualities, not just as soldiers but as charismatic leaders. Yet it remains true that the situation in the fourth century was made for great men as the situation in the fifth century was not. Diodoros, when he gets to 360 in his narrative of Greek history, declares for the first time that he thinks that when this can possibly be done a historian should shape his books around the deeds performed by a single man. He devotes his sixteenth book to Philip and his seventeenth to Alexander. Not only does he not manage this at any earlier point in his history, but he does not manage it in any later book either.

Not that later Greek history is quite like fifth-century Greek history. The Greek city-states never again enjoyed the sort of autonomy which they enjoyed even in the fifth century. Third-century Greek cities lived under the shadow of one or other of the dynasties which ruled Alexander's empire – the Attalids with their capital at Pergamon, the Seleucids with their capital further east, the Ptolemies with their capital at Egyptian Alexandria – or of the continuing Macedonian kingdom itself. But if controlling one's own foreign policy was now a fantasy even for the largest city, controlling one's own city was not. In cities that had been Greek for a long time, and also in many that had only newly become Greek, participatory civic structures were established, magistrates elected, laws passed, and rituals observed. The presence of powerful rulers who might intervene, or could be called upon for help, and who needed to be humoured, certainly made a difference to the way in which cities behaved, but the patterns of civic life continued – and would continue even after the Roman conquest of Greece at the beginning of the second century BC. We saw that already in the gymnasiarchy law from Beroia which I quoted in the first chapter.

One thing that distinguishes the cities of hellenistic Greece from earlier Greek cities is their propensity for writing up their decisions. Athens had acquired the 'epigraphic habit' in the fifth century, but elsewhere the habit was slower to catch on. From the hellenistic world, however, we have a very large corpus of public inscriptions, and from cities of every size and nature. The picture these reveal often betrays their date, either by explicit reference to the hellenistic kings or by the prominence of individual benefactors bailing out cities. But other inscriptions show the structures of civic life almost completely unchanged. I end with one such inscription, which records the decision of two small Greek cities to unite as one city.

Sympoliteia agreement between Stiris and Medeon in Phocis (Austin *Hellenistic World* no. 134, trans. Austin):

God. Good fortune. When Zeuxis was general of the Phocians, in the seventh month, convention between the city of Stiris and the city of Medeon. The Stirians and Medeonians have formed a single city, with their sanctuaries, their city, their territory, their harbours, all unencumbered [= none of these facilities have been mortgaged], on the following conditions: the Medeonians are all to be Stirians, equal and enjoying the same rights; they shall take part in the same assembly and the same elections for magistracies as the city of Stiris, and those who reach the proper age shall judge all the cases which come before the city; a *hierotamias* shall be appointed from among the Medeonians who shall offer the traditional sacrifices for

---

the Medeonians which are specified in the law of the city, together with the archons established at Stiris. The *hierotamias* shall receive the money which the archons [in Medeon] used to receive, half a mina and the share of the contributions to religious festivals which falls to the *hierotamias*. The *hierotamias* shall judge together with the archons the suits which the archons judge, and he shall draw lots for the courts if it is necessary to draw lots with the archons. It shall not be compulsory for those Medeonians to hold magistracies in Stiris who in Medeon have been archons, judges of foreigners, collectors of debts, *demiourgoi*, priests, high priests, and among women those who have held priesthoods, unless someone undertakes them willingly. Magistracies shall be filled from the Medeonians who have not performed public functions and from the Stirians. The administration of the sanctuaries at Medeon shall be carried out as required by the laws of the city. The territory of Medeon shall be all Stirian and the territory of Stiris shall all be Medeonian and jointly owned. The Medeonians shall participate in all the sacrifices at Stiris and the Stirians in all the sacrifices at Medeon. It shall not be permissible for the Medeonians to break away from the Stirians nor for the Stirians from the Medeonians. Whichever of the two sides does not abide by the written agreement shall pay to the side which does ten talents and they shall be liable to prosecution. The convention shall be inscribed on a stele and dedicated in the sanctuary of Athena, and a sealed copy of the convention shall be deposited with a private individual. The convention is with Thrason of Lilaia. Witnesses: Thrason son of Damatrias of Elatea, Eupalidas son of Thrason of Lilaia, Timokrates son of Epinicus of Tithorea. The Stirians shall give to the phratry of the Medeonians within four years five minas of silver and the place called Damatrea.

Were it not for external evidence, in the form of the nature of the inscription and its letter forms, this text would be virtually impossible to date on internal grounds. These were not communities simply going through the empty forms of traditional actions, but communities whose daily fortunes were still very much in their own hands and which were taking practical measures to ensure their own survival and prosperity.

For those for whom Greek history is a history of events, the events at Medeon and Stiris are trivial, and only the kings of the hellenistic world can be held to be makers of such history. But the great events of Greek history had never impinged very heavily on most of the inhabitants of Greek cities, and their hellenistic lives were not so very different from the lives of their classical predecessors. Not only did the modes of civic life forged in the archaic period in small self-governing poleis continue to be the framework upon which life in Greece was hung, but the pattern of expectations established in the Greek mainland was spread both to the territories conquered by Alexander to the east, and to the territories of the Roman conqueror to the west. And just as our expectations in literature, in philosophy, and in the visual arts have been shaped by the 'classical tradition' established in those strange communities with their outlandish ways, so too our own expectations of proper civic self-government owe much to the tedious local regulations that fill up so many stone inscriptions in the cities of the hellenistic Greek world.

Further reading

General

Two recent edited collections provide a more systematic analysis of Greek history: Cartledge (1998), Osborne (2000a).

1 Familiar but exotic: why Greece needs history

On Greek athletics see Golden (1998), Kyle (1987), Harris (1964), Gardiner (1930). For experimental assessment of the efficiency of athletic nudity see Instone (1990). For the images of the 'Perizoma group' see Shapiro (2000). For athletic nudity see McDonnell (1991), Arieti (1975). On desire and the gymnasium see Scanlon (2002) 199–273. On the Carpenter Painter's vase see von Bothmer (1986), Waddell (1991). On ligaturing of male genitals see Lissarrague (1990), Osborne (1997b); the most extensive study is Dingwall (1925). Dingwall's further interests are indicated by the titles of some of his other publications: *How to go to a medium* (London, 1927), *The Girdle of Chastity, a medico-historical study* (London, 1931), *Artificial Cranial Deformation* (Cambridge, 1933), *How to use a large library* 2nd edn

(Cambridge, 1933), and, co-authored with others, *The Haunting of Barley Rectory* (London, 1956), *The American Woman, a historical study* (London, 1956).

The psykter by Douris and other pictures of revelling satyrs are discussed in Bérard (1989). For satyrs' desire for women see Osborne 1996c. For images of victorious athletes see Kephalidou (1996).

The foundational texts in the modern study of Greek homo-sexuality are Dover (1978), Foucault (1985).

On Alcibiades' sexual activity see Gribble (1999) 73–7. On parallel constructions of homosexual and heterosexual desire see Davidson (1997) Part II Desire ch. 3 'Women and boys'. For the behaviour of Ischomachos' wife in later life see Harvey (1984).

The question of what constituted rape for Athenians is discussed by Omitowoju (2002).

The evidence of Aeschines 1 for Athenian law about pros-titution is discussed by Dover (1978) ch. 1, Fisher (2001). The idea of sexual behaviour being governed by 'protocols' comes from Winkler (1990).

The gymnasiarchy law from Beroia is Austin no. 118 and fully discussed in Gauthier and Hatzopoulos (1993). I discuss the relations between beards and the naked body in classical Greek art in Osborne (1997b).

On the Olympic games generally see Finley and Pleket (1976). On the early history of Olympia see Morgan (1990). For numbers of dedications see Snodgrass (1980) table at p. 53. On the relationship between sanctuaries and cities in the eighth century see the influential study of de Polignac (1995) and see further below ch. 7.

On the glory to be won from athletic victory and the special power that victory gave to athletes see Fontenrose (1968), Bohringer (1979) and especially Kurke (1993). On prizes at the Panathenaia see *IG* ii^2 2311 and Neils (1992); on prizes more generally see Young (1984). Euthymos is discussed by Currie (2002).

The criticisms of the luxurious life of the athlete are part of a wider attack on luxury, for which see Kurke (1992), Davidson (1997).

2 Inventing the Greek polis

My discussion of Pithekoussai is largely indebted to Ridgway (1992); see also D'Agostino (1999). Pithekoussai is further discussed in chapter 3. For Etruscan Italy see Spivey and Stoddart (1990), Barker and Rasmussen (1998). On early ships see Wallinga (1992).

Nestor's cup is ML 1; see also Jeffery (1961/1990) 235–6. Curse tablets are collected by Gager (1992) and discussed by Faraone (1991). Faraone (1996) discusses the cup of Nestor further. Early metrical writing is collected by Powell (1991) who argues that the alphabet was created to write down Homeric epic. See also the survey of early writing in Whitley (2001) 128–33, 188–91. For the use and spread of writing see Thomas (1992).

On Lefkandi see Popham et al. (1979, 1980, 1993); on the other sites mentioned (Zagora and Hypsile on Andros, Koukounaries on Paros, Xombourgo on Tenos, Agios Andreas on Siphnos) see Mazarakis-Ainian (1997), Lemos (2002).

On the late date at which a category of 'myth' separable from history was created see Detienne (1986) and, on Herodotus, Osborne (2002). On the stories of Trojan War heroes travelling in the central and western Mediterranean, see Malkin (1998).

For studies of Greek settlement abroad premised on the assumption that the classical pattern of settlement foundation reflected in the stories of early colonisation was the pattern really followed in those foundations see Graham (1964), Malkin (1987). For the example of the Athenian decision to send a colony to Brea see ML no. 49 (translated in Osborne (2000b) no. 232). For an alternative view of Greek settlement abroad, partially anticipated by Finley (1976), see Snodgrass (1994), Osborne (1998), Yntema (2000) and compare Dougherty (1993). For more general context compare Lyons and Papadopoulos (2002).

On Hekataios and early Greek history writing see Fowler (1996), Luraghi (2001). The clearest and most interesting case of Herodotus repeating a story and explicitly declaring that repeating it does not oblige him to believe it is at 7.152.

On oral traditions generally see Tonkin (1992) and Carsten (1995). For pioneering studies of oral tradition in the Greek world see Davies (1984) and Thomas (1989). I develop Davies arguments about the tradition on the foundation of Cyrene in Osborne (1996a) 8–17. The 'kernel' theory of tradition dies hard; for a recent reassertion see Malkin (2003).

The inscription to which Thucydides refers at 6.54.7 survives: ML no. 11. For the context and the ways in which the Athenians reinvented themselves see Loraux (1986).

The inscriptions recording the Theran ambassador's visit to Cyrene and the text of the oath which they claim had been sworn when the settlers were dispatched is ML no.5 (translated at Fornara (1983) no.18). For a recent discussion of the history of Cyrene see Mitchell (2000).

On Pausanias see Habicht (1985), Arafat (1996), Alcock, Cherry, and Elsner (2001), and Alcock (2002). For the influence of Pausanias on the archaeology of Attica see Camp (2001) index s.v. Pausanias.

3 How many Greeks were there and how did any of them survive?

My discussion of Pithekoussai is based on Ridgway (1992) 101–3. The Egyptian data are collected and discussed by Bagnall and Frier (1994) (p. 105 for death rate). On deficiency diseases see Garnsey (1999) ch. 4. For Soranus' description of rickets see *Gunaikeia* 2.43–4; for effective and ineffective (the manure of a land-crocodile, vitriolic copper and the bile of a hyena) cures for eye-disease see Herophilos *On Eyes* frg. 260. For the skeletal evidence from Metapontum see M. Henneberg and R.J. Henneberg (1998); for the debate over syphilis in antiquity see Sallares (1991) 282–3.

For general discussion of ancient demography and its consequences see Parkin (1992), Saller (1994). For the issue of who
the women were at Pithekoussai see Buchner (1975), Shepherd
(1999). For discussions of Greek ethnicity more generally see
Hall (1997), (2002).

For food needs see Foxhall and Forbes (1982), Garnsey
(1999) 19–21; Henneberg (1998) 513. Survival demands 2,000
kcalories a day for an adult, 1,500 for a child; active adults need
more like 2,900 kcals; 1 kg of wheat provides 3,330 kcals. On
different sorts of wheat see Sallares (1991).

On ancient agricultural productivity the truth is likely to
lie between the pessimism of Sallares (1991) 372–89 and the
optimism of Osborne (1987) 44–7. For the amount of farmland
on Pithekoussai see Caro (1994).

On burials and population in eighth-century Athens see
Morris (1987) with further comments by Osborne (1996a) 78–81.
The classic discussion of the population of classical Athens is
Gomme (1933); for the best recent discussions see Hansen (1986),
(1988). For Koressia on Keos see Cherry et al. (1991) 235–7.
The best discussion of the amount of Attica that was cultivated
is Garnsey (1985).

The most influential modern analysis of the Greek economy
is Finley (1973). Osborne (1987) provides a picture of the
ancient economy much closer to Finley's than that offered here.
I have come to believe that that picture is mistaken. On
Xenophon's *Ways and Means* see Gauthier (1976); on Xenophon's
Oikonomikos see Pomeroy (1994).

For the importance of items not vital for subsistence in the
archaic economy see Foxhall (1998). The evidence of transport
amphoras is discussed by Dupont (1998), Whitbread (1995)
and Koehler (1981). The evidence from the distribution of fine
pottery is discussed by Osborne (1996b). For a more general
picture of the long history of interconnectedness in the ancient
Mediterranean see Horden and Purcell (2000), ch. 9. For legal
agreements between cities see Gauthier (1972).

4 Law, tyranny and the invention of politics

For general introductions to the topics in this chapter see Murray (1980) 58–62, ch. 9, ch. 11; Osborne (1996a) 185–97, 215–25, 271–85.

For three rather different approaches to early Greek law see Gagarin (1986) with Wallace and Westbury (1989), Hölkeskamp (1992) and Thomas (1995). Drako's homicide law is ML 86 (Fornara (1983) 15B), the Dreros law ML 2 (Fornara (1983) 11), the Tiryns law is discussed at Osborne (1996a) 186–7, the Chios law is ML 8 (Fornara (1983) 19) and the Spartan *rhetra* is quoted by Plutarch *Life of Lykourgos* 6.1–8.

Solon's law on wills is quoted most completely by Demosthenes 46.14; evidence that it was notorious in the classical period is provided by the allusion to it at [Aristotle] *Constitution of the Athenians* 9.1–2 (and compare 35.2).

The classic, and very readable, account of early Greek tyranny remains Andrewes (1956). More recent discussions have put more emphasis on 'tyranny stories'. See, for example, Vernant (1982), Sourvinou-Inwood (1988), McGlew (1993). Archilochos pronounces on Gyges and tyranny in frg. 19 (W). Compare frg. 23.17–21 (W). Herodotus' account of Gyges, Kandaules and Kandaules' wife is at 1.8–14. Herodotus discusses tyranny at Corinth at 3.48–53 as well as at 5.92. The story about Myron of Sikyon comes from a quotation from a much later historian, Nikolaos of Damascus, writing at the time of the Roman emperor Augustus (*FGH* 90 F61).

On warfare in the *Iliad* and its relation to later warfare van Wees (1994), Morris (1987) 195–201, Greenhalgh (1973) chs 4 and 5, Pritchett (1971–91) Part IV, van Wees (2000). See also below, ch. 5.

On links between warfare and tyranny, see Snodgrass (1964) esp. chs 8–9, Salmon (1977), Cartledge (1977) and (2000), and van Wees (1995).

On Solon's property classes see Foxhall (1997). The laws are collected in Ruschenbusch (1966). For the case in favour of a 'code' see Osborne (1997a).

5 Making enemies

For introductions to Greek warfare see Connor (1988), Hanson (1989/2000), (1991), Pritchett (1971–91), Spence (1993), van Wees (2000).

On Sparta's archaic wars see Forrest (1968); on Sparta and Tegea see Boedeker (1993), Buxton (1994) ch. 10. The nature of the tradition about Sparta and Messenia has recently re-emerged as a topic for debate. For the older discussion see Pearson (1962), Starr (1965); for the recent revival see Alcock (2001), (2002) 132–75, and Luraghi (2002).

On Phokis and its wars see Ellinger (1993), McInerney (1999).

On the invention and early history of coinage see Howgego (1995) ch. 1; on its Lydian link see Xenophanes at Pollux *Onomasticon* 9.83; on its spread see Osborne (1996a) 250–59.

On the history of Persia see Frye (1984) 87–135, Cook (1983), Briant (1996), Brosius (2000). On the Ionian tyrants and Persia see Austin (1990).

On the Ionian Revolt see Murray (1988), Neville (1979).

For the value of exercises in counterfactual history see Ferguson (1997).

On the Persian Wars see Lazenby (1993), Burn (1984), Hignett (1963), Brunt (1953–4).

For Persia and Greece in the aftermath of the Persian Wars see Miller (1997).

On the Athenian empire see Meiggs (1972). The main sources are collected in Osborne (2000b). On the Athenian navy and issues of finance, see Gabrielsen (1994). The workings of Athenian empire and Peloponnesian League, as well as the nature of the conflict between Athens and Sparta, are discussed in detail in de Ste Croix (1972).

6 The city of freedom and oppression

Modern discussion of freedom in relation to ancient Greece has been dominated by German scholars (see Raaflaub (1985),

Ehrenberg (1967), Pohlenz (1966)), but in the past decade there has been much interest also in the Anglo-American world. Some of that interest (Patterson 1991) has been directed at personal liberty, but political freedom is the subject of forthcoming work by R.W. Wallace and P. Liddel. As Liddel in particular points out, it was George Grote in his great mid-nineteenth-century *History of Greece* who made Pericles' funeral oration central to the understanding and exposition of Athenian liberty.

Our understanding of politics at the end of the sixth century in Athens depends upon Herodotus 5.66, 69–70 and [Aristotle] *Constitution of the Athenians* 20–1. For an introduction to modern discussions see Osborne (1996a) 292–394. The issue of participation in Athenian democracy is discussed by Sinclair (1988). The particular issues of the demographics of Athenian democracy are explored by Hansen (1986) (esp. 51–64); compare Osborne (1985) 42–6.

The workings of law courts are described by [Aristotle] *Constitution of the Athenians* 63–9. For a recent discussion of the evidence, including archaeological, see Boegehold (1995). Our best evidence for the numbers of Athenian officials in the fifth century also comes from [Aristotle] *Constitution of the Athenians* 24.3. Evidence of age and wealth qualifications at Athens comes, for the Council from Xenophon, *Memorabilia* 1.2.35; for the courts from [Aristotle] *Constitution of the Athenians* 63.3–4; for the archons from [Aristotle], *Constitution of the Athenians* 7.4, 26.2; and for the Treasurers of Athena from [Aristotle], *Constitution of the Athenians* 47.1. On learning politics locally in the demes see Osborne (1990), (1985), Whitehead (1986).

For comparison of Athenian and modern democracy see Finley (1973), Ober and Hedrick (1996). On political theory in classical Athens see Farrar (1988), Raaflaub (1990). Protagoras' views are expounded in Plato *Protagoras* 320c–328c. For the difficulty of imagining all citizens as equal, see Aristotle *Politics* 1277b33–1278a26.

For the relationship between the growth of liberty and growth of slavery see Finley (1959), Patterson (1991), Osborne

(1995). On Greek slavery generally see Garlan (1988), Fisher (1993). For the lists of the property confiscated from those guilty of mutilating the herms and profaning the mysteries see ML 79 (Fornara (1983) 147D). For Lysias' father's workshop, see Lysias 12.19; for Demosthenes' father's workshops see Demosthenes 29.24. For Xenophon on mines see *Ways and Means* 4.13–15. For the Erechtheum workers see Randall (1953). On Pasion, Apollodoros and Phormio, see Davies (1971) 427–42, and on Apollodoros as an orator see Trevett (1992). The importance of slaves' status being marked by the treatment of their bodies is also brought out in Demosthenes 22.55: 'Indeed, if you wanted to contrast the slave to the free man, you would find the most important distinction in the fact that slaves are responsible in person.' For abuse of slaves in comedy see Aristophanes *Peace* 729–52, *Wasps* 439f., *Birds* 760. See also Weiler (2002). On Aristotle and 'natural slavery' see Garnsey (1996) 11–14, 107–27, Schofield (1990). For Aristotle's will see Diogenes Laertius *Lives of the Philosophers* 5.11–16. On slaves in warfare see Hunt (1998). On Spartan helots see below, ch. 7.

On Athenian metics see Whitehead (1977). The evidence for Athenian citizenship grants is collected in Osborne (1981–3). On women as *politides* at Athens see Patterson (1986); on women in Athens more generally see the classic article by Gould (1980); on women in ancient Greece and in Greek literature see Just (1989), Schmitt-Pantel (1992), Reeder (1995). On women and religion in Aristophanes see Bowie (1993); on Lysistrata see Lewis (1955). For Plato's women 'guardians' see *Republic* 5.451c–e. For the potential power of women within the household see Foxhall (1989).

On the nature of Greek religion see Gould (1985); a very useful survey of work on Greek religion is provided by Bremmer (1994/1999). On women and cult generally see Dillon (2002). On the exclusion of men/women from religious life: see Osborne (1994a), and on women and offerings see Osborne (1994b). The religious calendar of the Athenian state is discussed by Parker (1996) 43–55; the calendar of the Athenian demes by Parker (1987). Examples of calendars of city, phratry, *genos* and deme are to be found as RO nos. 1, 37, 62 and 63. Images of sacrifice are collected by van Straten (1995). For sacrifice and meat see Jameson (1988). On the Panathenaia in general see Neils (1992). On the religious obligations of Athens' allies in the Delian League see the evidence collected in Osborne (2000b) 97–101.

7 The unity and diversity of the Greek city

Particularly useful as an introduction to classical literature because of its emphasis on the context is Taplin (2000). Our information about Thucydides' daughter comes from Marcellinus' *Life of Thucydides* 43:

> Some say that the eighth book of the *History* is not genuine. For it is not by Thucydides, but some say it is by his daughter and some that it is by Xenophon. I respond to these that it is clearly not by his daughter. For it does not belong to the female nature to imitate such skill and excellence, and secondly if she had been such a woman, she would not have made every effort to conceal herself, she would not have written the eighth book alone but would also have left many other books, showing off her own nature. That it is not by Xenophon the character of the book practically cries out.

The variety of constitutional arrangements within the Greek city can be reviewed in detail in Jones (1987) and Rhodes with Lewis (1997).

On the Spartan mirage see Ollier (1933–4), Kennell (1995), Hodkinson (2000) ch. 2. On Spartan helots see Finley (1975), Hodkinson (2000) ch. 4, Ducat (2002), de Ste Croix (1972/2002). For comparison between helots and other slaves see Cartledge (1985). On the Spartan constitution see Andrewes (1966/2002). On Agesilaos see Cartledge (1987).

On election by lot Headlam (1891) remains valuable, but see now Cordano and Grottanelli (2001). For the election of generals at Athens see Piérart (1974). For the fifth-century Boiotian constitution we have the unique advantage of a surviving literary description in chapter 16 of the surviving fragment of a history of the early fourth century known as *Hellenica Oxyrhynchia*.

On the question of the unity of Greek law see Todd and Millett (1990) 7–11. For striking divergences compare women's property rights: Schaps (1979). For issues involving building contractors see Burford (1969) and RO no. 60. On international conventions with regard to war see Pritchett (1971–91) vol. 5 ch. 3 on treatment of war captives, vol. 4 ch. 2 on war dead. The clearest ancient statement of the conventions governing conduct in war is in Diodoros 30.18.2.

On Greek views of the powers of the dead see Johnston (1999). On Greek burial customs see Kurtz and Boardman (1971). For the Selinous law see Jameson, Jordan and Kotansky (1993); for the Cyrene law see RO 97. Curse tablets are usefully collected in Gager (1992): see no. 43 for a particularly interesting example in this context.

On the spaces of religious activity see Scully (1962), de Polignac (1995), Osborne (1987) ch. 8, Alcock and Osborne (1994). Classical archaeologists have been most interested in certain types of temple, and hence there is no good survey of the variety of temple buildings archaeologically attested. For a traditional take on Greek temples see Coldstream (1985).

For the Ptoon *kouroi* see Ducat (1971); for the *korai* from the Athenian Acropolis see Payne and Young (1950); for *kouroi* and *korai* more generally see Richter (1968), (1970); for the offerings at Emborio see Morgan (1990) 230–33.

On the Greek alphabet, its regional variations and its development see Jeffery (1961/1990). On the history of the Greek language see Horrocks (1997). The varieties of early Greek pottery are well displayed in Boardman (1998). On the diffusion of Attic drama see Taplin (1999).

8 Was Alexander the end of Greek history?

For introductions to fourth-century history see Osborne ed. (2000a) ch. 8; Hornblower (2002) chs 15–19. On Sparta in the early fourth century see Cartledge (1987). For the prospectus of the so-called 'Second Athenian Confederacy' see RO 22. The prevailing modern accounts of the Second Athenian Confederacy arguably exaggerate its virtues, see Marshall (1905), Cargill (1981). On the Theban hegemony of the fourth century see Buckler (1980). On military developments see van Wees (2000) and, for an introduction to the history of fortifications, Osborne (1987) ch. 7.

On the ethnicity of the Macedonians and the question of competition in the Olympic games see Hall (2002) 154–6, 165–6. On Philip see Ellis (1976), Cawkwell (1978). On Philip's polygamy see Ogden (1999) 17–27. Of all the numerous books on Alexander, the most reliable of recent guides is provided by Bosworth (1988). On Alexander's behaviour in India see Bosworth (1996).

On the crisis of the polis see Runciman (1990). On political organisation outside Athens and Sparta see Brock and Hodkinson (2000).

On the successors to Alexander, and the hellenistic world generally, see Shipley (2000), and on the immediate successors in detail Bosworth (2002). For the ways in which Greek cities dealt with hellenistic rulers (and vice versa) see Ma (1999). A good range of inscriptional evidence for hellenistic cities is represented in Austin (1981).

Bibliography

Alcock, S. (2001) 'The peculiar Book IV and the problem of the Messenian past' in Alcock, Cherry and Elsner (2001) 142–53.

—— (2002) *Archaeologies of the Greek Past. Landscape, Monuments, and Memories*, Cambridge: Cambridge University Press.

Alcock, S. and R. Osborne ed. (1994) *Placing the Gods. Sanctuaries and Sacred Space in Ancient Greece*, Oxford: Oxford University Press.

Alcock, S., J. Cherry and J. Elsner ed. (2001) *Pausanias. Travel and Memory in Roman Greece*, Oxford: Oxford University Press.

Andrewes, A. (1956) *The Greek Tyrants*, London: Hutchinson.

—— (1966/2002) 'The government of classical Sparta' in E. Badian ed. *Ancient Society and Institutions*, Oxford: Blackwell. Reprinted in Whitby (2002) 49–68.

Arafat, K. (1996) *Pausanias' Greece: Ancient Artists and Roman Rulers*, Cambridge: Cambridge University Press.

Arieti, J. (1975) 'Nudity in Greek athletics', *Classical World* 68: 431–6.

Austin, M.M. (1981) *The Hellenistic World from Alexander to the Roman Conquest*, Cambridge: Cambridge University Press.

—— (1990) 'Greek tyrants and the Persians 546–479 BC', *Classical Quarterly* 40: 289–306.

Bagnall, R.S. and B.W. Frier (1994) *The Demography of Roman Egypt*, Cambridge: Cambridge University Press.

Barker, G. and T. Rasmussen (1998) *The Etruscans*, Oxford: Blackwell.

Bérard, C. (1989) *A City of Images*, Princeton: Princeton University Press.

Boardman, J. (1998) *Early Greek Vase Painting*, London: Thames and Hudson.

Boedeker, D. (1993) 'Hero cult and politics in Herodotus: the bones of Orestes' in Dougherty and Kurke (1993) 164–77.

Boegehold, A. (1995) *The Athenian Agora*. Vol. 28. *The Lawcourts*, Princeton: American School of Classical Studies.

Bohringer, F. (= F. de Polignac) (1979) 'Cultes d'Athlètes en Grèce classique: propos politique, discours mythique', *Revue des études anciennes* 81: 5–18.

Bosworth, A.B. (1988) *Conquest and Empire. The Reign of Alexander the Great*, Cambridge: Cambridge University Press.

—— (1996) *Alexander and the East. The Tragedy of Triumph*, Oxford: Oxford University Press.

—— (2002) *The Legacy of Alexander: Politics, Warfare, and Propaganda under the Successors*, Oxford: Oxford University Press.

Bothmer, D. von (1986) 'An archaic red-figured kylix', *The J. Paul Getty Museum Journal* 14: 5–20.

Bowie, A.M. (1993) *Aristophanes. Myth, Ritual and Comedy*, Cambridge: Cambridge University Press.

Bremmer, J.N. (1994/1999) *Greek Religion*, Greece and Rome New Surveys in the Classics No. 24. Oxford: Oxford University Press.

Briant, P. (1996) *Histoire de l'Empire perse: de Cyrus à Alexandre*, Paris: Fayard.

Brock, R.W. and S. Hodkinson ed. (2000) *Alternatives to Athens. Varieties of Political Organization and Community in Ancient Greece*, Oxford: Oxford University Press.

Brosius, M. (2000) *The Persian Empire from Cyrus II to Artaxerxes I*, LACTOR 16, London: LACTOR.

Brunt, P.A. (1953–4) 'The Hellenic League against Persia', *Historia* 2 135–63, reprinted in Brunt (1992) 47–83.

—— (1992) *Studies in Greek History and Thought*, Oxford: Oxford University Press.

Buchner G. 1975 'Nuovi aspetti e problemi posti degli scavi di Pitecusa con particulari considerazioni sulle oreficerie de stile orientalizzante antico' in *Contribution à l'étude de la société eubéennes.* Cahiers du Centre Jean Bérard II: 59–86. Naples.

Buckler, J. (1980) *The Theban Hegemony, 371–362 BC*, Cambridge, Mass.: Harvard University Press.

Burford, A. (1969) *The Greek Temple Builders at Epidauros*, Liverpool: Liverpool University Press.

Burn, A.R. (1984) *Persia and the Greeks*, revised edition, London: Duckworth.

Buxton, R. (1994) *Imaginary Greece*, Cambridge: Cambridge University Press.

—— ed. (2000) *Oxford Readings in Greek Religion*, Oxford: Oxford University Press.

Camp, J.M. (2001) *The Archaeology of Athens*, London: Thames and Hudson.

Cargill, J. (1981) *The Second Athenian League. Empire or Free Alliance?* Berkeley: University of California Press.

Caro, S. de (1994) 'Appunti per la topographia della chora di Pithekoussai nella prima età coloniale', in *Apoikia: scritti in onore de Giorgio Buchner, Annali del' Instituto Orientale di Napoli* n.s.1 (1994) 37–46.

Carsten, J. (1995) 'The politics of forgetting: migration, kinship and memory on the periphery of the southeast Asian state', *Journal of the Royal Anthropological Institute* n.s. 1: 317–35.

Cartledge, P.A. (1977) 'Hoplites and heroes', *Journal of Hellenic Studies* 97: 11–27.

—— (1985) 'Rebels and sambos in classical Greece: a comparative view' in P. Cartledge and F.D. Harvey ed. *Crux*, London: Duckworth, 1–15.

—— (1987) *Agesilaos and the Crisis of Sparta*, London: Duckworth.

Cartledge, P.A. ed. (1998) *Cambridge Illustrated History: Ancient Greece*, Cambridge: Cambridge University Press.

Cartledge, P.A. (2000) 'The birth of the hoplite' in P.A. Cartledge, *Spartan Reflections*, London: Duckworth.

Cartledge P.A., and F.D. Harvey (1985) *Crux*, London: Duckworth.

Cawkwell, G.L. (1978) *Philip of Macedon*, London: Faber and Faber.

Cherry, J.F, J. Davis, and E. Mantzourani (ed.) (1991) *Landscape Archaeology as Long-term History. Northern Keos in the Cycladic Islands*, Los Angeles: UCLA Institute of Archaeology.

Coldstream, J.N. (1985) 'Greek temples: why and where?' in P. Easterling and J. Muir ed. *Greek Religion and Society*, Cambridge: Cambridge University Press, 67–97.

Connor, W.R. (1988) 'Early Greek warfare as symbolic expression', *Past and Present* 119: 3–29; reprinted in Osborne (2004).

Cook, J.M. (1983) *The Persian Empire*, London: Dent.

Cordano F. and C. Grottanelli (2001) *Sorteggio pubblico e cleromanzia dall' Antichità all' età moderna*, Milan: Edizioni Et.

Currie, B. (2002) 'Euthymus of Locri: a case study in heroization in the classical period', *Journal of Hellenic Studies* 103: 24–44.

D'Agostino, B. (1999) 'Euboean colonisation in the Gulf of Naples' in G. Tsetskhladze ed. *Ancient Greeks West and East*, Leiden: Brill, 207–27.

Davidson, J. (1997) *Courtesans and Fishcakes. The Consuming Passions of Classical Athens*, London: Harper Collins.

Davies, J.K. (1971) *Athenian Propertied Families*, Oxford: Oxford University Press.

—— (1984) 'The reliability of oral tradition' in J.K. Davies and L. Foxhall ed. *The Trojan War: Its Historicity and Context*, Bristol: Bristol Classical Press, 87–110.

Detienne, M. (1986) *The Creation of Mythology*, Chicago: Chicago University Press.

Dillon, M. (2002) *Women and Girls in Classical Greek Religion*, London: Routledge.

Dingwall, E.J. (1925) *Male Infibulation*, London: John Bale, Sons and Danielsson Ltd.

Dougherty, C. (1993) *The Poetics of Colonization. From City to Text in Archaic Greece*, Oxford: Oxford University Press.

Dougherty, C. and L. Kurke ed. (1993) *Cultural Poetics in Archaic Greece*, Cambridge: Cambridge University Press.

Dover, K.J. (1978) *Greek Homosexuality*, London: Duckworth.

Ducat, J. (1971) *Les Kouroi du Ptoion: Le sanctuaire d'Apollon Ptoieus à l'époque archaïque*, Paris: de Boccard.

—— (2002) 'The obligations of helots' in Whitby (2002) 196–211.

Dupont, P. (1998) 'Archaic East Greek trade amphoras' in R.M. Cook and P. Dupont *East Greek Pottery*, London: Routledge, 142–91.

Ehrenberg, V. (1967) 'Freedom – ideal and reality' in *The Living Heritage of Greek Antiquity*, The Hague: Mouton: 132–46.

Ellinger P. (1993) *La légende nationale phocidienne. Artémis, les situations extrêmes et les récits de guerre d'anéantissement,* Bulletin de Correspondance Hellénique Suppl. 27. Paris.

Ellis, J.R. (1976) *Philip II and Macedonian Imperialism*, London: Thames and Hudson.

Faraone, C. (1991) 'The agonistic context of early Greek binding spells' in C. Faraone and D. Obbink ed. *Magika Hiera. Ancient Greek Magic and Religion*, Oxford: Oxford University Press, 3–32.

—— (1996) 'Taking the "Nestor's Cup Inscription" seriously: erotic magic and conditional curses in the earliest inscribed hexameters', *Classical Antiquity* 15: 77–112.

Farrar, C. (1988) *The Origins of Democratic Thinking*, Cambridge: Cambridge University Press.

Ferguson, N. ed. (1997) *Virtual History. Alternatives and Counterfactuals*, London: Picador.

Finley, M.I. (1959) 'Was Greek civilization based on slave labour?', *Historia* 8: 145–64, reprinted in M.I. Finley (1981) *Economy and Society of Ancient Greece*, London: Chatto and Windus.

—— (1973a) *The Ancient Economy* (2nd edition, 1985), Berkeley: University of California Press.

—— (1973b) *Democracy Ancient and Modern*, London: Chatto and Windus.

—— (1975) 'Sparta', in M.I. Finley, *The Use and Abuse of History*, London: Chatto and Windus, 161–78.

—— (1976) 'Colonies – an attempt at a typology', *Transactions of the Royal Historical Society* 26: 167–88.

Finley, M.I. and H.W. Pleket (1976) *The Olympic Games: The First Thousand Years*, London: Chatto and Windus.

Fisher, N. (1993) *Slavery in Classical Greece*, London: Duckworth.

—— (2001) *Aeschines* Against Timarchos, Oxford: Oxford University Press.

Fontenrose, J. (1968) 'The hero as athlete', *California Studies in Classical Antiquity* 1: 73–104.

Fornara, C.W. (1983) *Translated Documents of Greece and Rome vol.1 Archaic Times to the End of the Peloponnesian War*, Cambridge: Cambridge University Press.

Forrest W.G. (1968) *A History of Sparta*, London: Hutchinson.

Foucault, M. (1985) *The Use of Pleasure. The History of Sexuality,* vol. 2, London: Penguin.

Fowler R. (1996) 'Herodotos and his contemporaries', *Journal of Hellenic Studies* 116: 62–87.

Foxhall, L. (1989) 'Household, gender and property in classical Athens', *Classical Quarterly* 39: 32–44.

—— (1997) 'A view from the top: evaluating the Solonian property classes' in Mitchell and Rhodes (1997) 137–47.

—— (1998) 'Cargoes of the heart's desire. The character of trade in the archaic Mediterranean world' in N. Fisher and H. van Wees ed. *Archaic Greece. New Approaches and New Evidence*, London: Duckworth, 295–309.

Foxhall, L. and H. Forbes (1982) '*Sitometreia*: the role of grain as a staple food in antiquity', *Chiron* 12: 41–90.

Frye, R. (1984) *The History of Ancient Iran*, Munich: Beck.

Gabrielsen, V. (1994) *Financing the Athenian Fleet*, Baltimore: Johns Hopkins.

Gagarin, M. (1986) *Early Greek Law*, Berkeley: University of California.

Gager, J. (1992) *Curse Tablets and Binding Spells from the Ancient World*, Oxford: Oxford University Press.

Gardiner, E.N. (1930) *Athletics of the Ancient World*, Oxford: Oxford University Press.

Garlan, Y. (1988) *Slavery in Ancient Greece*, Ithaca: Cornell University Press.

Garnsey, P.D.A. (1985) 'Grain for Athens' in Cartledge and Harvey (1985) 62–75; reprinted with addendum by W. Scheidel in Garnsey (1998) 183–200.

—— (1996) *Ideas of Slavery from Aristotle to Augustine*, Cambridge: Cambridge University Press.

—— (1998) *Cities, Peasants and Food in Classical Antiquity*, Cambridge: Cambridge University Press.

—— (1999) *Food and Society in Classical Antiquity*, Cambridge: Cambridge University Press.

Gauthier, P. (1972) *Symbola*: *les étrangers et la justice dans les cités grec-ques*, Nancy: Université de Nancy.

—— (1976) *Un commentaire historique des Poroi de Xénophon*, Paris: University de Nancy II.

Gauthier, P. and M.B. Hatzopoulos (1993) *La loi gymnasiarchique de Beroia*, Paris: De Boccard.

Golden, M (1998) *Sport and Society in Ancient Greece*, Cambridge: Cambridge University Press.

Goldhill S. and R. Osborne ed. (1999) *Performance Culture and Athenian Democracy*, Cambridge: Cambridge University Press.

Gomme, A.W. (1933) *The Population of Athens in the Fifth and Fourth Centuries BC*, Oxford: Oxford University Press.

Gould, J. (1980) 'Law, custom and myth: aspects of the social position of women in classical Athens', *Journal of Hellenic Studies* 100: 38–59; reprinted in Gould (2001) 112–57.

—— (1985) 'On making sense of Greek Religion' in P. Easterling and J. Muir *Greek Religion and Society* (Cambridge) 1–33 reprinted in Gould (2001) 203–34.

—— (2001) *Myth, Ritual, Memory, and Exchange. Essays in Greek Literature and Culture*, Oxford: Oxford University Press.

Graham, A.J. (1964) *Colony and Mother City* (2nd edn 1983), Manchester: Manchester University Press/Chicago: Chicago University Press.

Greenhalgh, P. (1973) *Early Greek Warfare. Horsemen and Chariots in the Homeric and Archaic Ages*, Cambridge: Cambridge University Press.

Gribble, D. (1999) *Alcibiades and Athens. A Study in Literary Presentation*, Oxford: Oxford University Press.

Habicht, C. (1985) *Pausanias' Guide to Ancient Greece*, Berkeley: University of California Press.

Hall, J.M. (1997) *Ethnic Identity in Greek Antiquity*, Cambridge: Cambridge University Press.

—— (2002) *Hellenicity. Between Ethnicity and Culture*, Chicago: University of Chicago Press.

Hansen, M.H. (1986) *Demography and Democracy. The Number of Athenian Citizens in the Fourth Century BC*, Herning: Systime.

—— (1988) *Three Studies in Athenian Demography*, Copenhagen: Det Kongelige Danske Videnskabernes Selskab.

Hanson V.D. ed. (1991) *Hoplites. The Classical Greek Battle Experience*, London: Routledge.

Hanson, V.D. (1989/2000) *The Western Way of War. Infantry battle in classical Greece*, 2nd edition, Oxford: Oxford University Press: Kongelige Danske Videnskabernes Selskab.

Harris, H.A. (1964) *Greek Athletes and Athletics*, London: Thames and Hudson.

Harvey, F.D. (1984) 'The wicked wife of Ischomachos', *Echos du monde classique* 28: 68–70.

Headlam, J.W. (1891) *Election by Lot at Athens*, Cambridge: Cambridge University Press.

Henneberg, M. and R.J., ed. (1998) 'Biological characteristics of the population based on analysis of skeletal remains' in J.C. Carter, *The Chora of Metaponto: The Necropoleis*, Austin: University of Texas Press, 503–56.

Hignett, C. (1963) *Xerxes' Invasion of Greece*, Oxford: Oxford University Press.

Hodkinson, S. (2000) *Property and Wealth in Classical Sparta*, London: Duckworth.

Hölkeskamp, K.-J. (1992) 'Written law in archaic Greece', *Proceedings of the Cambridge Philological Society* 38: 87–117.

Horden, P. and N. Purcell (2000) *The Corrupting Sea*, Oxford: Blackwell.

Hornblower, S. (2002) *The Greek World 479–323 BC*, 3rd edition. London: Routledge.

Horrocks, G.C. (1997) *Greek: A History of the Language and its Speakers*, London: Longman.

Howgego, C. (1995) *Ancient History from Coins*. London: Routledge.

—— (2002) *Ancient History from Coins*, London: Routledge.

Hunt, P. (1998) *Slaves, Warfare and Ideology in the Greek Historians*, Cambridge: Cambridge University Press,

Instone, S. (1990) 'The naked truth about Greek athletics', *Omnibus* 20.

Jameson, M.H. (1988) 'Sacrifice and animal husbandry in classical Greece' in C.R. Whittaker ed. *Pastoral Economies in Classical Antiquity*, Cambridge: Proceedings of the Cambridge Philological Society Supplementary Volume, 87–119.

Jameson, M.H., D. Jordan and R. Kotansky (1993) *A Lex Sacra from Selinous* (Greek Roman and Byzantine Studies Monographs 11).

Jeffery, L.H. (1961/1990) *Local Scripts of Archaic Greece*, Oxford: Oxford University Press.

Johnston S.I. (1999) *Restless Dead. Encounters between the Living and the Dead in Ancient Greece*, Berkeley: University of California Press.

Jones, N.F. (1987) *Public Organization in Ancient Greece*, Philadelphia: American Philosophical Society.

Just, R. (1989) *Women in Athenian Law and Life*, London: Routledge.

Kennell, N. (1995) *The Gymnasium of Virtue: Education and Culture in Ancient Sparta*, Chapel Hill: University of North Carolina Press.

Kephalidou, E. (1996) ΝΙΚΗΤΗΣ. Εικονογραφική μελέτη του αρχαίου ελληνικού αθλητισμού. Thessaloniki: Aristoteleio Panepistemio Thessalonikes.

Koehler, C.G. (1981) 'Corinthian developments in the study of trade in the fifth century', *Hesperia* 50: 449–58.

Kurke, L. (1992) 'The Politics of ἁβροσύνη in archaic Greece', *Classical Antiquity* 11: 90–121.

—— (1993) 'The economy of *kudos*' in Dougherty and Kurke (1993) 131–63.

Kurtz, D.C. and J. Boardman (1971) *Greek Burial Customs*, London: Thames and Hudson.

Kyle, D.G. (1987) *Athletics in Ancient Athens*, Leiden: Brill.

Lazenby, J.F. (1993) *The Defence of Greece 490–479B.C.*, Warminster: Aris and Phillips.

Lemos, I. (2002) *The Protogeometric Aegean*, Oxford: Oxford University Press.

Lewis, D.M. (1955) 'Who was Lysistrata?', *Annual of the British School at Athens* 50: 1–12; reprinted in D.M. Lewis (1997) *Selected Papers in Greek and Near Eastern history*, Cambridge: Cambridge University Press, 187–202.

Lissarrague, F. (1990) 'The sexual life of satyrs' in D. Halperin, J.J. Winkler, and F. I. Zeitlin ed. *Before Sexuality. The Construction of Erotic Experience in the Ancient Greek World*, Princeton: Princeton University Press, 53–81.

Loraux, N. (1986) *The Invention of Athens*, Cambridge, Mass.: Harvard University Press.

Luraghi, N. (2002) 'Becoming Messenian', *Journal of Hellenic Studies* 122: 45–69.

—— ed. (2001) *The Historian's Craft in the Age of Herodotus*, Oxford: Oxford University Press.

Lyons, C.L. and J.K. Papadopoulos (2002) *The Archaeology of Colonialism*, Malibu: J. Paul Getty Museum.

Ma, J. (1999) *Antiochos III and the Cities of Western Asia Minor*, Oxford: Oxford University Press.

Malkin, I. (1987) *Religion and Colonization in Ancient Greece*, Leiden: Brill.

—— (1998) *The Returns of Odysseus. Colonization and Ethnicity*, Berkeley: University of California Press.

—— (2002) 'Exploring the validity of the concept of "Foundation": a visit to Megara Hyblaia', in V. Gorman and E. Robinson ed. *Oikistes. Studies in Constitutions, Colonies, and Military Power in the Ancient World, Offered in Honor of A.J. Graham*, Leiden: Brill, 195–225.

—— (2003) 'Tradition in Herodotus: the foundation of Cyrene', in P.S. Derow and R.C.T. Parker ed. *Herodotus and his World*, Oxford: Oxford University Press, 153–70.

Marshall, F.H. (1905) *The Second Athenian Confederacy*, Cambridge: Cambridge University Press.

Mazarakis-Ainian, A. (1997) *From Rulers' Dwellings to Temples. Architecture, Religion and Society in Early Iron Age Greece (1100–700 BC)*, Jonsered: Åstrom.

McDonnell, M. (1991) 'The introduction of athletic nudity: Thucydides, Plato, and the vases', *Journal of Hellenic Studies* 111: 182–93.

McGlew, J.F. (1993) *Tyranny and Political Culture in Ancient Greece*, Ithaca: Cornell University Press.

McInerney, J. (1999) *The Folds of Parnassos. Land and Ethnicity in Ancient Phokis*, Austin: University of Texas.

Meiggs, R. (1972) *The Athenian Empire*, Oxford: Oxford University Press.

Miller, M.C. (1997) *Athens and Persia in the Fifth Century BC A Study in Cultural Receptivity*, Cambridge: Cambridge University Press.

Mitchell, B. (2000) 'Cyrene: typical or atypical?' in R. Brock and S. Hodkinson ed. *Alternatives to Athens. Varieties of political organization and community in ancient Greece*, Oxford: Oxford University Press, 82–102.

Mitchell, L.G. and P.J. Rhodes ed. (1997) *The Development of the* Polis *in Archaic Greece*, London: Routledge.

Morgan, C.A. (1990) *Athletes and Oracles. The Transformation of Olympia and Delphi in the Eighth Century BC*, Cambridge: Cambridge University Press.

Morris, I.M. (1987) *Burial and Ancient Society. The Rise of the Greek City-state*, Cambridge: Cambridge University Press.

Murray, O. (1980) *Early Greece*, 2nd edition: 1993, London: Fontana.

—— (1988) 'The Ionian Revolt', *Cambridge Ancient History* ed. 2 Vol.4, 461–90.

Murray, O and S. Price ed. (1990) *The Greek City from Homer to Alexander*, Oxford: Oxford University Press.

Neils, J. ed. (1992) *Goddess and Polis. The Panathenaic Festival in Ancient Athens*, Princeton: Princeton University Press.

Neville, J. (1979) 'Was there an Ionian revolt?', *CQ* 29 268–75.

Ober, J. and C. Hedrick (1996) *Demokratia. A Conversation on Democracies, Ancient and Modern*, Princeton: Princeton University Press.

Ogden, D. (1999) *Polygamy, Prostitutes and Death: The Hellenistic Dynasties*, London: Duckworth.

Ollier, F. (1933–4) *Le mirage spartiate: étude sur l'idéalisation de Sparte dans l'antiquité grecque*, 2 vols, Paris: de Boccard.

Omitowoju, R. (2002) *Rape and the Politics of Consent in Classical Athens*, Cambridge: Cambridge University Press.

Osborne, M.J. (1981–3) *Naturalization in Athens*, 4 vols. Brussels: Koninklijke Academie voor Wetenschappen, Letteren en Schone Kunsten van België.

Osborne, R. (1985) *Demos. The Discovery of Classical Attika*. Cambridge: Cambridge University Press.

—— (1987) *Classical Landscape with Figures*, London: George Philip.

—— (1990) 'The Demos and its divisions' in Murray and Price (1990) 265–94.

—— (1994a) 'Women and sacrifice in classical Greece', *Classical Quarterly* 43: 392–405; reprinted in Buxton (2000) 294–313.

—— (1994b) 'Looking on Greek style. Does the sculpted girl speak to women too?' in I.M. Morris ed. *Classical Greece: Ancient Histories and Modern Archaeologies*, Cambridge: Cambridge University Press, 81–96.

—— (1995) 'The economics and politics of slavery at Athens', in A. Powell ed. *The Greek World*, London: Routledge, 27–43.

—— (1996a) *Greece in the Making 1200–c.479 BC*, London: Routledge.

—— (1996b) 'Pots, trade and the archaic Greek economy', *Antiquity* 70: 31–44.

—— (1996c) 'Desiring women on Athenian pottery' in N.B. Kampen ed. *Sexuality in Ancient Art*, Cambridge: Cambridge University Press.

—— (1997a) 'Law and laws: how do we join up the dots?' in Mitchell and Rhodes (1997) 74–82.

—— (1997b) 'Men without clothes: heroic nakedness and Greek art' in M. Wyke ed. *Gender and the Body in Mediterranean Antiquity*, Oxford: Blackwell, 80–104 (= *Gender and History* 9: 504–28).

—— (1998) 'Early Greek colonization? The nature of Greek settlement in the West' in N. Fisher and H. van Wees ed. *Archaic Greece. New Approaches and New Evidence*, London: Duckworth, 251–70.

—— (2002) 'Archaic Greek History' in E.J. Bakker, I.J.F. De Jong, and H. Van Wees ed. *Brill's Companion to Herodotus*, Leiden, Brill, 497–520.

—— ed. (2000a) *Classical Greece. Short Oxford History of Europe. Vol. 1*, Oxford: Oxford University Press.

—— ed. (2000b) *The Athenian Empire*. LACTOR 1 4th edition. London: LACTOR.

Parker, R.C.T. (1987) 'Festivals of the Attic demes' in T. Linders and G. Nordquist *Gifts to the Gods*, Stockholm: Academia Usaliensis.

—— (1996) *Athenian Religion: A History*, Oxford: Oxford University Press.

Parkin, T. (1992) *Demography and Roman Society*, Baltimore: Johns Hopkins University Press.

Patterson, C. (1986) '*Hai attikai*: the other Athenians', *Helios* 13: 49–67.

Patterson, O. (1991) *Freedom*. Vol.1, *Freedom in the Making of Western Culture*. London: Tauris.

Payne, H. and G.M. Young (1950) *Archaic Marble Sculpture from the Athenian Acropolis*, revised edition, London: Cresset Press.

Pearson, L. (1962) 'The pseudo-history of Messenia and its authors', *Historia* 11: 397–426.

Piérart, M. (1974) 'À propos de l'élection des stratèges athéniennes', *Bulletin de Correspondence Hellénique* 98: 125–46.

Pohlenz, M. (1966) *Freedom in Greek Life and Thought: The History of an Ideal* (German edition 1955), Dordrecht: Reidel.

Polignac, F. de (1995) *Cults, Territory and the Origins of the Greek City-state* (first French edition, 1984), Chicago: University of Chicago Press.

Pomeroy, S. (1994) Xenophon *Oikonomikos*, Oxford: Oxford University Press.

Popham, M.R. et al. (1979, 1980, 1993) *Lefkandi I*, 2 vols; *Lefkandi II.2*, London: British School at Athens.

Powell A. ed. (1995) *The Greek World*, London: Routledge.

Powell, B.B. (1991) *Homer and the Origin of the Greek Alphabet*, Cambridge: Cambridge University Press.

Pritchett W.K. (1971–91) *The Greek State at War*, 5 vols, Berkeley: University of California Press.

Raaflaub, K. (1985) *Entdeckung der Freiheit: zur historischen Semantik und Gesellschaftsgeschichte eines politischen Grundbegriffes der Griechen*, Munich: Beck.

Raaflaub, K. (1990) 'Contemporary perceptions of democracy in fifth-century Athens' in J.R. Fears ed. *Aspects of Athenian Democracy*, Copenhagen: Museum Tusculanum Press, 33–70.

Randall, R.H. (1953) 'The Erechtheum workmen', *American Journal of Archaeology* 57: 199–210.

Reeder, E.D. ed. (1995) *Pandora. Women in Classical Greece*, Princeton: Princeton University Press.

Rhodes, P.J. with D.M. Lewis (1997) *The Decrees of the Greek States*, Oxford: Oxford University Press.

Richter, G.M.A. (1968) *Korai: Archaic Greek Maidens*, London: Phaidon.

—— (1970) *Kouroi: Archaic Greek Youths*, 3rd edn, London: Phaidon.

Ridgway, D. (1992) *The First Western Greeks*, Cambridge: Cambridge University Press.

Runciman, W.G. (1990) 'Doomed to extinction: the *polis* as an evolutionary dead-end' in Murray and Price (1990) 347–67.

Ruschenbusch, E. (1966) ΣΟΛΩΝΟΣ ΝΟΜΟΙ, Historia Einzelschriften 9.

Sallares, R. (1991) *The Ecology of the Ancient Greek World*, London: Duckworth.

Saller, R.P. (1994) *Patriarchy, Property and Death in the Roman Family*, Cambridge: Cambridge University Press.

Salmon, J. (1977) 'Political hoplites', *Journal of Hellenic Studies* 97: 84–101.

Scanlon, T.F. (2002) *Eros and Greek Athletics*. Oxford: Oxford University Press.

Schaps, D.M. (1979) *Economic Rights of Women in Ancient Greece*, Edinburgh: Edinburgh University Press.

Schmitt-Pantel, P. ed. (1992) *A History of Women. Vol.1 From Ancient Goddesses to Christian Saints*, Cambridge, Mass.: Harvard University Press.

Schofield, M. (1990) 'Ideology and philosophy in Aristotle's theory of slavery' in G. Patzig ed. *Aristoteles' 'Politik', Akten des XI Symposium Aristotelicum*, Göttingen: Vandenhoeck of Puprecht, 1–27.

Scully, V. (1962) *The Earth, the Temple and the Gods: Greek Sacred Architecture*, New Haven: Yale University Press.

Shapiro, H.A. (2000) 'Modest athletes and liberated women: Etruscans on Attic black-figure vases' in B. Cohen ed. *Not the Classical Ideal: Athens and the Construction of the Other in Greek Art*, Leiden: Brill, 313–37.

Shepherd, G. (1999) 'Fibulae and females: intermarriage in the western Greek colonies and the evidence from cemeteries' in G.R. Tsetskhladze ed. *Ancient Greeks West and East*, Leiden: Brill, 267–300.

Shipley, G. (2000) *The Greek World after Alexander, 323–30 BC*, London: Routledge.

Sinclair, R.K. (1988) *Democracy and Participation in Athens*, Cambridge: Cambridge University Press.

Snodgrass, A.M. (1964) *Early Greek Armour and Weapons*, Edinburgh: Edinburgh University Press.

—— (1980) *Archaic Greece. The Age of Experiment*, London: Dent.

—— (1994) 'The growth and standing of the early western colonies' in F. de Angelis and G. Tsetskhladze ed. *The Archaeology of Early Greek Colonization*, Oxford: Oxbow, 1–10.

Sourvinou-Inwood, C. (1988) '"Myth" and history: on Herodotos 3.48 and 50–53', *Op. Ath.* 17: 167–82.

Spence, I. (1993) *The Cavalry of Classical Greece. A Social and Military History*, Oxford: Oxford University Press.

Spivey, N. and S. Stoddart (1990) *Etruscan Italy. An Archaeological History*, London: Batsford.

Starr, C.G. (1965) 'The credibility of early Spartan history', *Historia* 14: 257–72; reprinted in Whitby (2002) 26–42.

Ste Croix, G.E.M. de (1972) *The Origins of the Peloponnesian War*, London: Duckworth.

—— (1972/2002) 'The helot threat' in Whitby (2002) 190–95; reprinted from de Ste Croix (1972).

Taplin, O. P. (1999) 'Spreading the word through performance' in Goldhill and Osborne (1999) 33–57.

—— (2000) *Literature in the Greek and Roman Worlds: A New Perspective*. Oxford: Oxford University Press.

Thomas, R. (1989) *Oral Tradition and Written Record in Classical Athens*, Cambridge: Cambridge University Press.

—— (1992) *Literacy and Orality in Ancient Greece*, Cambridge: Cambridge University Press.

—— (1995) 'Written in stone? Liberty, equality, orality and the codification of law', *Bulletin of the Institute of Classical Studies* 40: 59–74; reprinted in L. Foxhall and A. Lewis ed. (1996) *Greek Law in its Political Setting*, Oxford: Oxford University Press, 9–32.

Todd, S.C. and P.C. Millett (1990) 'Law, society and Athens' in P. Cartledge, P. Millett and S.C. Todd ed. *Nomos. Essays in Athenian Law, Politics, and Society*, Cambridge: Cambridge University Press, 1–18.

Tonkin, E (1992) *Narrating our Pasts. The Social Construction of Oral History*, Cambridge: Cambridge University Press.

Trevett, J.C. (1992) *Apollodoros Son of Pasion*, Oxford: Oxford University Press.

van Straten, F.T. (1995) *Hiera Kala. Images of Animal Sacrifice in Archaic and Classical Greece*, Leiden: Brill.

van Wees, H. (1994) 'The Homeric way of war: the *Iliad* and the hoplite phalanx I', *Greece and Rome* 41: 1–18.

—— (1995) 'Politics and the battlefield. Ideology in Greek warfare' in Powell ed. (1995) 153–78.

—— (2000) 'The city at war' in Osborne ed. (2000a) 81–110.

Vernant, J.-P. (1982) 'From Oidipous to Periander: lameness, tyranny, incest in legend and history', *Arethusa* 15: 19–38.

Waddell, G (1991) 'The Greek pentathlon' in *Greek Vases in the J. Paul Getty Museum* 5: 99–106.

Wallace, R.W. and Westbury, R. (1989) 'Review of Gagarin *Early Greek Law*', *American Journal of Philology* 110: 362–7.

Wallinga, H.T. (1992) *Ships and Sea-power before the Great Persian War*, Leiden: Brill.

Weiler, I. (2002) 'Inverted *kalokagathia*' in T. Wiedemann and J. Gardner ed. *Representing the Body of the Slave*, London: Frank Cass, 11–28.

Whitbread, I.K. (1995) *Greek Transport Amphorae. A Petrological and Archaeological Study*, Athens: British School at Athens.

Whitby, M. ed. (2002) *Sparta*, Edinburgh: Edinburgh University Press.

Whitehead, D. (1977) *The Ideology of the Athenian Metic*, Proceedings of the Cambridge Philological Society Supplementary Volume. Cambridge: Cambridge Philological Society.

—— (1986) *The Demes of Attica*, Princeton: Princeton University Press.

Whitley, J. (2001) *The Archaeology of Greece*, Cambridge: Cambridge University Press.

Winkler, J.J. (1990) *The Constraints of Desire*, London: Routledge.

Yntema, D. (2000) 'Mental landscapes of colonization: the ancient written sources and the archaeology of early colonial-Greek southeastern Italy', *Bulletin Antieke Beschaving* 75: 1–50.

Young, D.C. (1984) *The Olympic Myth of Amateur Athletics*, Chicago: Chicago University Press.

Index